Law and Evil

ELGAR STUDIES IN LEGAL THEORY

Series Editor: Wojciech Sadurski, *Sydney Law School, University of Sydney, Australia*

Elgar Studies in Legal Theory is a new series designed to cultivate and promote high quality works of scholarship on all aspects of legal theory. The focus of the series is on the development of original thinking in legal theory, with topics ranging from law and language, logic and legal reasoning, morality and the law, critical legal studies, and transnational law. Innovative work is encouraged from both established authors and the new generation of scholars.

Titles in this series include:

Understanding the Nature of Law
A Case for Constructive Conceptual Explanation
Michael Giudice

Comparative Law as Critique
Günter Frankenberg

Law's Political Foundations
Rivers, Rifles, Rice, and Religion
John O. Haley

Authority in Transnational Legal Theory
Theorising Across Disciplines
Edited by Roger Cotterrell and Maksymilian Del Mar

Legal Conversation as Signifier
Jan M. Broekman and Frank Fleerackers

Technology and the Trajectory of Myth
David Grant and Lyria Bennett Moses

Legal Theory and the Media of Law
Thomas Vesting

Gender, Alterity and Human Rights
Freedom in a Fishbowl
Ratna Kapur

Law and Evil
The Evolutionary Perspective
Wojciech Załuski

Law and Evil

The Evolutionary Perspective

Wojciech Załuski

Full Professor, Department of Philosophy of Law and Legal Ethics, Jagiellonian University, Krakow, Poland

ELGAR STUDIES IN LEGAL THEORY

Edward Elgar
PUBLISHING

Cheltenham, UK • Northampton, MA, USA

Published by
Edward Elgar Publishing Limited
The Lypiatts
15 Lansdown Road
Cheltenham
Glos GL50 2JA
UK

Edward Elgar Publishing, Inc.
William Pratt House
9 Dewey Court
Northampton
Massachusetts 01060
USA

A catalogue record for this book
is available from the British Library

Library of Congress Control Number: 2018944740

This book is available electronically in the **Elgar**online
Law subject collection
DOI 10.4337/9781786436504

FSC
www.fsc.org
MIX
Paper from
responsible sources
FSC® C013056

ISBN 978 1 78643 649 8 (cased)
ISBN 978 1 78643 650 4 (eBook)

Typeset by Columns Design XML Ltd, Reading
Printed and bound in Great Britain by TJ International Ltd, Padstow

This book is dedicated to the memory of my beloved Father, Jan Załuski (1944-2012), my truest – loving, patient, and wise – teacher of philosophy as a way of life.

Contents

Introduction

Once we begin to look at the discussions pursued within legal philosophy, we shall notice that rarely are attempts made to connect – either directly or indirectly – claims about the nature of law and evolutionary–anthropological assumptions (with a few exceptions, such as the works of Friedrich August von Hayek or Mauro Barberis, who was developing Hayek's cultural-evolutionist approach). This state of affairs does not seem to be satisfactory. Arguably, reflection on human nature inspired by evolutionary biology may substantially enrich discussions about the law. This book is intended to be a modest contribution in this direction. Its main purpose is twofold: to reconstruct an evolutionary view of human nature and to examine through the prism of this view two legal–philosophical problems, viz. the problem of the (historical) evolution of law and the controversy between *ius*-naturalists (the adherents of natural law doctrine) and legal positivists. The title of this book – *Law and Evil* – is justified by the fact that in my reconstruction of the evolutionary view of human nature I shall put special stress on the problem of the sources of human propensity for evildoing.

Since the term 'evil' lacks clarity, some disambiguation is necessary at the outset. In its narrower sense this term is applied only to the most extreme, most serious forms of intentional wrongdoing (evil in a broader sense). They can be understood in three different ways. First, extreme evil (that is, evil in a narrower sense) may consist in doing evil just for the sake of doing evil. This is the so-called 'absolute evil'. On this understanding, the harm done need not be very serious for a wrongdoer to be called 'absolutely evil'; it suffices that he is doing an evil act, even a relatively minor one (such as stealing pears – St Augustine's famous autobiographical example), just because this act is evil. He is indifferent to the suffering of other people involved, that is, he does not share the suffering but also does not derive any pleasure form it; what may give him pleasure (as a side effect) is the very fact of violating moral rules, and this violation becomes for him an end in itself.

Second, extreme evil may consist in sadistic wrongdoing, that is, deriving pleasure from making the other person suffer. In this case an agent does not commit evil for the sake of evil but in order to derive pleasure from the sight of the other person's – the victim's – suffering. One can call this variety of extreme evil 'sadistic evil'.

On the third understanding, an act is extremely evil if it causes 'considerable harm to a victim' and 'is done for no intelligible reason', and as such (that is, being done without any intelligible reason) is found by people to be 'extremely perplexing' (Feinberg 2002: 144). Each of the above three forms of extreme evil – absolute, sadistic and, as one may call it, 'unintelligible' – can be dubbed 'demonical' or 'pure'. These definitions are, of course, sketchy. But they are sufficient for the purpose of formulating one of the important theses of this book, viz. that human nature, as it was shaped by biological evolution, is free from proclivities to extreme (absolute, sadistic, or unintelligible) evil. However, it is not free from proclivities to less extreme forms of wrongdoing. It is with respect to them that I shall use the term 'evil'. Its meaning in this book is therefore general: it is, basically, equivalent to 'intentional wrongdoing'. However, I propose to distinguish within this broad category more specific kinds of evil, viz. primary and secondary. I shall clarify their sense in the course of the following summary of the book's content.

In Chapter 1 I shall argue for the claim that (Darwinian) evolutionary theory leads to the view of human nature which I call 'doubly ambivalent'. The *first ambivalence* of human nature is that it comprises immoral, neutral and moral tendencies. The *second ambivalence* is that our natural (shaped by natural selection) moral tendencies are far from being *genuinely* moral. They embrace, in broad outline, the tendency to feel empathy, kin altruism, tribalism and reciprocal altruism (tendency to act in accordance with the tit-for-tat strategy). In other words: evolutionary ethics is fourfold – it is composed of ethics of empathy, family (kin altruism) ethics, tribal ethics and tit-for-tat (reciprocal altruism) ethics. By evolutionary ethics I understand a set of moral rules expressive of (or correlated with) moral tendencies shaped by natural selection, and by genuine ethics a set of moral rules which impose much stronger requirements of impartiality than evolutionary ethics (a more precise account of genuine ethics will be provided in the course of my analyses). Accordingly, I defend the claim that biological evolution endowed us with moral tendencies, but there is a discontinuity between these tendencies and genuine ethics. I shall also use a distinction between primary and secondary evil. By 'primary evil' I shall understand evil actions which flow from our immoral tendencies, and by 'secondary evil', evil actions which flow from our neutral or moral tendencies. Secondary evil can be viewed as an undesirable (from the perspective of genuine ethics) consequence of our evolutionarily shaped neutral and moral tendencies;

the notion of secondary evil therefore makes sense only on the assumption that there is some more 'pure' type of ethics than the one 'built into' our biological nature. It should be stressed that the distinction between 'primary' and 'secondary' evil only points at the main source of a given immoral action. It does not imply that secondary evil is less evil – is a less serious form of wrongdoing – than 'primary' evil; it may indeed be true that, as a rule, primary evil is more reprehensible, but, certainly, there are many exceptions. It should also be noticed that the same immoral action (for example, killing) can be caused by immoral tendencies (for example, envy or egoism), neutral ones (for example, hierarchical propensities) or moral ones (for example, group or kin altruism).

Chapter 2 provides an interpretation of the history of law from the anthropological perspective offered in this book: it is argued that the history can be interpreted as a process of overcoming evolutionary ethics and moving closer to genuine ethics. In the early stages of the history of law, legal rules had a twofold character: (1) they counteracted our immoral tendencies; (2) and they were almost fully expressive of our moral tendencies shaped by natural selection. Accordingly, even though they counteracted primary evil, they generated (and also constituted) secondary evil, because the moral tendencies of which they were expressive are, as mentioned, morally ambivalent, and as such give rise to an inferior form of ethics. The core of legal systems which appeared in the course of the history has not substantially changed: all, or almost all, of them have contained rules against murder, theft, fraud, and so on, which are necessary for the stability of social orders. But both the form of these rules and the other (noncore) rules underwent a serious change, which can be interpreted as a radical departure from evolutionary ethics. The progress of law can therefore be viewed as reflecting a transition from rudimentary – evolutionary – ethics to genuine ethics. This general account of the progress of law is developed in Chapter 2 in two stages. In the first stage I present a progression towards moral egalitarianism, and in the second stage I discuss more specific progressive tendencies of criminal and civil law.

Chapter 3 deals with the implications of the evolutionary view of human nature for the controversy between *ius*-naturalists and legal positivists. The argument I propose proceeds in two steps. In the first step I argue that the deep divergence between evolutionary ethics and genuine ethics may be plausibly interpreted as an argument for metaethical (moral) realism, that is, for the thesis that ethical (deontic and axiological) judgements possess truth values. In the second step I argue that even though metaethical realism is not contradictory to legal positivism, it better harmonizes with *ius*-naturalism than with legal positivism.

This book deals with the problem of the implications of the evolutionary view of human nature for questions of legal philosophy – a problem which I previously tackled in my 2009 book for the same publisher, *Evolutionary Theory and Legal Philosophy*. On the one hand, the present book can be viewed as a continuation of the analyses pursued in the earlier one, since it tackles *different* legal–philosophical questions: of the relevance of the evolutionary view of human nature for the understanding of the historical development of law and for the controversy between theories of natural law and legal positivism. On the other hand, it departs from the earlier book in an important point – that of understanding human nature: the picture I defend in this book is less optimistic than the one I outlined in *Evolutionary Theory and Legal Philosophy*. This fact explains the perspective assumed in this book, which is focused on the origins and varieties of human evil. The two pictures are, in fact, not mutually contradictory; in my opinion, the new one is simply more complete and, as such, enables one to tackle *new* questions, which my previous (more optimistic) view of human nature made rather difficult to answer. In particular, I previously argued that law is an expression of our cooperative tendencies, and thereby should not be viewed as counteracting human nature. This overly sweeping claim, however, is difficult to reconcile with the profound changes that legal systems have undergone since the dawn of human history. The picture offered in this book, as I hope to show, allows a plausible analysis of these changes. It does not deny the claim that large parts of legal systems can be regarded as expressions of human nature (its moral – cooperative – tendencies) but implies that this is only a part of the truth; one gains a more nuanced account of law (and of its evolution) if one assumes a more ambivalent view of human nature, especially if a distinction is made between evolutionary ethics and genuine ethics (which I have already drawn in *Evolutionary Theory and Legal Philosophy*, but not sharply enough). Needless to say, the problem of philosophical interpretation of the results of evolutionary theory is a complex one; other reconstructions of the evolutionary view of human nature than the one proposed here are possible (given, so to say, the philosophical indeterminacy or open-endedness of scientific theories). My goal was to provide an interpretation which is consistent with scientific knowledge and philosophically fruitful, that is, capable of shedding light on our everyday experiences and on the history of moral and legal systems.

One final remark is in order. At the beginning of this Introduction I mentioned that Friedrich August von Hayek invoked evolutionary theory in his analyses of law. I do not examine his theory in this book, however, as much of *Evolutionary Theory and Legal Philosophy* dealt with its evaluation, and especially with critical evaluation of his scepticism regarding the usefulness of evolutionary biology in the context of the social sciences (his approach, as already mentioned, was cultural-evolutionist, not biological-evolutionist). I do not wish to repeat my conclusions, which remain unchanged and which need not be invoked in the context of problems I examine in this book.

Some of the ideas proposed in this book (respectively, in Chapter 1, section 4.1., Chapter 1, section 2.1., and Chapter 2, section 3.1.) have already been presented in the form of three articles: 'On Three Types of Empathy: The Perfect, the Truncated, and the Contaminated' (2007), *Logos i Ethos*, 2(45), 1–16; 'The Varieties of Egoism. Some Reflections on Moral Explanation of Human Action' (2016), in: B. Brożek, M. Heller and M. Hohol (eds), *The Concept of Explanation*, Krakow: Copernicus Center Press, Krakow, 263–77; 'The Psychological Bases of Primitive Egalitarianism. Reflections on Human Political Nature' (2016), in: J. Stelmach, B. Brożek and Ł. Kurek (eds), *The Emergence of Normative Orders*, Krakow: Copernicus Center Press, 83–106. I have drawn some materials from these articles, with substantial modifications.

1. The double ambivalence of human nature

1. THE EVOLUTIONARY VIEW OF HUMAN NATURE: NEITHER PESSIMISTIC NOR OPTIMISTIC

In the discussions concerning evolutionary theory's implications for the understanding of human nature, one can distinguish two extreme positions (cf. de Waal 2006). On the one hand, one may argue that human nature is amoral, lacking in moral dispositions; on the other, it may be considered that we come to the world with well-developed moral dispositions, and lacking in immoral dispositions.

Perhaps the most famous defence of the first, pessimistic, view was provided by Thomas Huxley in his 1894 essay *Evolution and Ethics*. He claimed that the characteristic feature of man is 'self-assertion, the unscrupulous seizing upon all that can be grasped, the tenacious holding of all that can be kept'; that man's behaviour 'is adjusted to cosmic strife [and] manifests ruthless and ferocious destructiveness when his anger is roused by opposition' (Huxley 1995 (1894): 129). This pessimistic picture of man was strictly connected with Huxley's gloomy view of the world; as he wrote, 'this world is full of pain and sorrow; grief and evil fall, like rain, upon both the just and unjust ... Brought before the tribunal of ethics, the cosmos might well seem to stand condemned. The conscience of man revolted against the moral indifference of nature' (Huxley 1995 (1894): 130). An even stronger version of this view was defended by George C. Williams, who asserted that natural selection is

> a process of maximizing short-sighted selfishness ... The survival of one organism is possible only at the great cost to others ... Huxley did not go far enough in his condemnation of the evolutionary process. We now have a far deeper understanding of evolution than Huxley had, and far more information on what this process has wrought. Huxley, for instance, understood nothing of forces favouring the development of nepotism or of parent–offspring and other sorts of conflict in nature. He knew little of the prevalence and violence of infanticide and cannibalism. (Williams 1995: 318)

The other extreme view – the optimistic one – assumes that biological evolution has endowed us with a number of prosocial instincts which directly lead to moral behaviour. Darwin (1871: 67) distinguished four such tendencies or instincts: 'taking pleasure in the society of one's fellows'; 'feeling sympathy for them'; 'performing various services for them'; and 'regarding others' approbation and disapprobation'. One cannot say, however, that Darwin assumed the optimistic view: he was deeply aware of the possibility of conflicts between social instincts and other instincts, for example the instincts of self-preservation, hunger, lust and vengeance (and also of the morally imperfect or incomplete character of the social instincts themselves). Nonetheless, his insight regarding the presence of prosocial instincts in human nature could have led other evolutionary thinkers, such as the famous anarchist philosopher Peter Kropotkin, to adopt the optimistic view.

It must be admitted, though, that of these two extreme views, the optimistic one was adopted much less frequently than the pessimistic. But both views seem to be implausible: they are onesided, failing to give justice to the complexity of human nature, its multilayered character. I shall argue that our 'evolutionary' nature can be most aptly characterized by the term 'double ambivalence'.

The view of human nature as doubly ambivalent is neither pessimistic nor optimistic; rather, it is a combination of both. This view is based on two claims. The first is that human nature comprises immoral tendencies (egoism, envy, aggression, self-deception), neutral tendencies (some emotions, hierarchical propensities, the desire for self-transcendence) and moral tendencies (empathy, kin and reciprocal altruism, tribalism). This is the *first ambivalence*: human nature is not monolithic in its moral fibre (though I do not insist that one could not find other examples of immoral, neutral or moral tendencies apart from the ones mentioned above and analysed in further parts of this chapter). The *second ambivalence*, more interesting than the first one, is that the moral tendencies themselves are morally imperfect (far from what constitutes or gives rise to what I call 'genuine ethics'), and thereby morally ambivalent. It is therefore not true (*contra* pessimists) that our nature does not determine any kind of morality: our nature comprises a number of moral tendencies whose 'correlates' are rules of what I call 'evolutionary ethics'. However, the morality determined by these tendencies is (*contra* optimists) very imperfect: it may lead to immoral behaviour, which I have called 'secondary evil'. Accordingly, human nature, *even in its better part*, constitutes our 'gravity' (*pesanteur*), in Simone Weil's sense (1988: 132) – that is, the force of the natural impulses of the soul, which we should oppose; for example, the impulse to seek moral equilibrium by taking revenge or by awaiting reward (cf. Weil 1988: 132). As Weil aptly remarks, it is not by chance that we speak about 'falling into' only in the context of evil; we cannot 'fall into' goodness, since goodness is something 'above' us, towards which we have to soar, overcoming our natural impulses, which drag us lower.

There is, however, an important optimistic element of the view of human nature defended in this book: the view implies that human nature does not contain *demonically* amoral tendencies, that is, human beings do not possess evolutionarily shaped tendencies to commit extreme evil – absolute, sadistic, or 'unintelligible'. In fact, the nonexistence of extremely evil proclivities is a simple corollary of the logic of biological evolution. A propensity can be a biological adaptation only if it increased our ancestors' biological fitness (the chances of survival and reproduction). But this biological goal, which each evolutionary adaptation must, by definition, serve, is, of course, ethically acceptable. Consequently, even immoral tendencies which were shaped by natural selection are not *totally* immoral, because they (ultimately) serve an ethically acceptable goal. One may query, however, how to reconcile this (optimistic) conviction with all too many testimonies to human cruelty: that cruelty *for its own sake* may be perpetrated by humans is a sad fact (cf. Zdziechowski 1993, or the memorable chapter about *violenza inutile* (useless violence) from Primo Levi's famous 1986 book *I sommersi e i salvati*, published two years later in English as *The Drowned and the Saved*). The simple answer to this question is that just as human beings are capable of going *above* their 'evolutionary ethics' (determined by their evolutionarily shaped moral tendencies) and reaching the stage of 'genuine ethics', so they may fall *below* this level. This is due to the fact that human beings, thanks to their reasoning capacities, may, so to say, free themselves (to a certain but considerable degree) from their biological nature not only in the right direction but also in the wrong one.

In the remainder of this chapter I shall develop at greater length the view of human nature as doubly ambivalent.

2. IMMORAL TENDENCIES

2.1 Egoism

In moral–psychological analyses, egoism is usually assumed to be a primitive, 'unanalysable' motive, that is, one which does not flow from some other more basic psychological phenomena. However, this widely accepted and apparently self-evident assumption seems to be mistaken. I shall argue that: (1) egoism is not a primitive motive but, rather, a manifestation of some more basic psychological phenomena; (2) one can distinguish three different forms of egoism depending on its psychological basis, viz., cognitively based, *hybris*-based and instinct-based; (3) two of these three forms of egoism (viz. cognitively based and instinct-based) can be plausibly viewed as a product of biological evolution.

In my analysis I shall assume a commonsense definition of egoism as an agent's tendency to pursue his own interests to an exceedingly high degree, that is, without duly respecting the other agents' interests. This definition presupposes that pursuing one's own interest is not in itself morally wrong – it becomes morally wrong only when it is done 'in an exceedingly high degree', and the degree of the morally legitimate – nonegoistic – pursuit of one's interest is determined by morality, which says how much respect is due to other people's interests in the course of pursuing one's own interest. Egoism can be defined equivalently in at least two different ways. Schopenhauer defined egoism as 'an urge to one's being and well-being' (*der Drang zum Dasein und Wohlsein*) (Schopenhauer 2009: 662; 2010: 196). This definition requires a slight correction, since, as already noted, not all types of care for oneself can be viewed as egoism. Egoism is an *excessive* 'urge to one's being and well-being' (an insufficient urge of this kind is abnegation). Egoism can also be defined by modifying the Evangelical precept 'love thy neighbour as thyself' (Mark 12:31; Matthew 22:39; Luke 10:27), which arguably states the conditions of the morally right conduct towards other people. Now, one can say that a person is egoist if and only if he loves himself more than his 'neighbour'. Thus, we have three arguably equivalent definitions of egoism: as an agent's tendency to pursue one's interests without duly respecting the other agents' interests, as an excessive 'urge to one's being and well-being' and as loving oneself more than one's 'neighbour'.

My basic claim is that egoism may flow from three different psychological sources: cognitive bias of egocentrism, *hybris*, and biological instincts of self-preservation and reproduction. Accordingly, one can distinguish three forms of egoism: cognitively based, *hybris*-based and instinct-based. I shall now present these three forms in more detail.

Cognitively based egoism flows from overestimating the 'reality' of oneself as compared with the 'reality' of others (that is, from egocentrism). For an agent who manifests this form of egoism, other people are substantially 'less real' than herself – or even 'unreal'. This conviction leads to a diminished capacity to consider other people's perspectives and to the tendency to interpret events with excessive reference to oneself. This account of egocentrism is somewhat different from, though related to, the ordinary type, according to which egocentrism is an excessive preoccupation with oneself, which may (but does not have to) result in not paying sufficient attention to or even completely neglecting the fact that other human beings have their own 'inner worlds'. Thus, on the ordinary account, an egocentric person does not necessarily downplay the 'reality' of other people (she is just excessively pre-occupied with herself), whereas on my account an egocentric person downplays the 'reality' of other people and, as a result, may (but does not have to) become excessively preoccupied with himself. Egocentrism (on my account) seems to be at least partly caused by the fact that we have direct access to our ego, to our mental life, and lack direct access to other people's egos, to their mental lives; other people's mental states (beliefs, emotions, attitudes) can only be known indirectly. This indirect character of our cognition of other people's mental states is particularly salient when such cognition takes the form of inferring (by analogical reasoning) those other people's mental states from their behaviour. But it occurs also when the cognition proceeds via *Einfühlung* (a kind of psychological insight into another person's mental state): even this form of cognition does not possess the 'directness' which is typical for self-knowledge. It is clear that the fact that we have privileged access to our own mental life does not have to lead to egoism, although it seems always to lead to the conviction that other people are somewhat less real than ourselves. We are all to some extent egocentric. This privileged access leads to egoism only if egocentrism assumes (for reasons to be ascertained by empirical psychology) the form of *strong* egocentrism, that is, if it generates in the agent a conviction that other people are *substantially* less real than himself or even unreal – that, figuratively speaking, the ontological status of other people resembles that of 'shadows' (regarded more as objects than as real persons). Thus, it is strong egocentrism, not egocentrism *simpliciter*, that underlies a cognitively based egoism.

Valuable insights into the phenomenon of egocentrism have been provided by social and cognitive psychologists who have identified and analysed in depth many of its manifestations, such as, for example, a cognitive bias called the 'spotlight effect' (cf. Gilovich, Medvec, Savitsky 2000). The spotlight effect consists in people's belief that they are noticed more than is really the case. They believe that they are in a 'social spotlight', overestimating their own importance to other people. This phenomenon is obviously egocentric in nature: since people are at the centre of their own world, they tend to believe that they are also at the centre – or close to the centre – of other people's worlds. In the case of the spotlight effect, overestimation of one's own 'reality' (which is characteristic of each manifestation of egocentrism) does not therefore lead to discounting the 'reality' of other people, but rather to overestimating the 'reality of oneself' in the consciousness of other people. The spotlight effect may be more or less acute for different people. It seems that those who manifest it particularly strongly are more likely than others to be subject to strong egocentrism, that is, to discounting the reality of other people, and in consequence to cognitively based egoism. I have discussed here only one egocentric 'effect' discovered by social and cognitive psychologists, but there are others too (some of them strictly connected with the spotlight effect), such as 'the illusion of transparency' (overestimation of the degree to which one's mental state is known by others); 'self-as-target bias' (the agent's belief that the course of events in the world is particularly 'inimical' to her own plans and intentions – more so than to the plans and intentions of other people); 'false consensus effect' (overestimation of the degree to which other people share one's beliefs and emotions); and the opposite effect, 'false uniqueness effect' (underestimation of the degree to which other people share one's beliefs and emotions).

By way of a historical digression, one may note that Schopenhauer (cf. 2009: 630) hinted at the claim that egoism may be a result of our having direct access only to our own mental life, and thereby seeing other people as 'representations'. He developed this insight in the spirit of the Upanishads, suggesting that the correct cognitive stance consists not in recognizing that other persons are real but in negating the reality of one's own ego. Cognitively based egoism can therefore be overcome in two different ways. The traditional ('Western') 'therapy' to work against it consists in recognizing that other people have the same – *full* – reality as oneself, whereas the Upanishads therapy (the 'Eastern' type) consists in recognizing that other people have the same – *none* – reality as oneself, and that the only reality is that of the 'cosmic ego' (Atman–Brahman). It is a matter of dispute whether the practical consequences of liberation from egoism are the same irrespective of which of these two anti-egoistic therapies one undergoes. One could argue that acceptance of the belief (endorsed by the Upanishads and Schopenhauer) that the reality of an individual ego is apparent may discourage one from performing acts of benevolence, because if other people's egos are unreal, it is unclear why one should care at all for the wellbeing of those other people. The fact that one's own ego is also unreal is not a plausible answer; it begs the question. The only plausible answer could be that all people are 'immersed' in the nonindividual ego (Atman–Brahman). But, following Max Scheler, one could ask whether beneficial acts thus motivated are not in fact a 'camouflaged egoism' (Scheler 1980: 78): if one helps another knowing that the other is in fact oneself (in accordance with the famous teaching of the Upanishads summarized in the phrase *Tat-Twam-Asi* or 'that art thou', that is, your individual ego hides at its depths – is identical with – the cosmic ego), then in helping others one in fact helps oneself. The above remarks also provide an answer to the question of whether cognitively based egoism is morally blameable. The answer is obviously in the affirmative, for the simple reason that this form of egoism is relatively easily avoidable: most people can overcome, by a relatively small mental effort, their impression of 'the lesser reality' of other people – in other words, they can easily overcome their egocentric proclivities or at least prevent them from turning into strong egocentrism and, consequently, into cognitively based egoism. The exception is to be made for those who suffer from some cognitive defect – some kind of a deficit of mental energy – that incapacitates them from overcoming their impression of the 'lesser reality' of other people. A precise description of this kind of defect belongs to the domain of psychopathology.

Instinct-based egoism is an excessive manifestation of biological instincts of self-preservation and reproduction. These instincts 'move' human beings to undertake actions serving the realization of their basic biological goals even if performing these actions means violating other people's morally justified interests. Of the three varieties of egoism, the instinct-based one is the most distinctly hedonistic (evolution 'has motivated' us to pursue our biological 'goals' through the promise of pleasure accompanying their realization). One can therefore say that a behavioural manifestation specific to this form of egoism consists in attaching undue importance to hedonistic values at the price of neglecting other – higher – values. We come to the world with this form of egoism present, and to overcome it is the fundamental purpose of education as well as of moral self-improvement. Clearly, these educational and self-improvement efforts are not always successful: instinct-based egoism becomes a dominant motive of action of many people. It is worth noting that it is this form of egoism that Immanuel Kant had in mind when he wrote about egoism (the tendency to prioritize self-interest over the interests of other people and over moral law) as the basic obstacle to our following moral rules, and thereby as a *conditio sine qua non* of the 'radical evil' (*das radikal Böse*) of human nature (cf. Kant 1986: 21–56). Thus, in Kant's view, egoism is at the root of human inability to unwaveringly follow moral principles (which is the essential content of his doctrine of 'radical evil', which I analyse in more detail at the end of this chapter).

Hybris-based egoism does not flow from the impression that other persons are substantially less real or unreal, but from the conviction that other persons are of lesser worth – that is, from *hybris*. *Hybris* is the belief in one's own superiority over other persons and in one's having special rights and privileges flowing from this purported superiority. It therefore implies a blatant denial of a fundamental moral equality of human beings. *Hybris* manifests itself as self-confidence bordering on arrogance, insolence, overbearing pride, self-aggrandizement. It is the opposite of humility and reverence, the latter being

> the virtue that keeps human beings from trying to act like gods, does not let them forget that they are humans ... An irreverent soul is arrogant and shameless, unable to feel awe in the face of things higher than itself. As a result, an irreverent soul is unable to feel respect for people it sees as lower than itself – ordinary people, prisoners, children. (Woodruff 2001: 3)

According to Aristotle, a particularly sharp manifestation of *hybris* is the deliberate humiliation of another person for no other reason than the pleasure involved. The cause of the pleasure of the *hybristic* man is that he finds himself greatly superior to others when ill-treating them. Thus, *hybris* manifests itself in an especially acute form when one gives offence neither for profit nor revenge, but simply because one delights in inflicting shame on others (cf. Elster 1999: 62–3, 173–8). Undoubtedly, *hybris*-based egoism is the most wrongful form of egoism, precisely because it flows from *hybris*, rightly regarded by the ancient Greeks as the most serious moral depravity and assumed in the Christian ethics (where it was called *superbia*) to be the most serious of human sins (and the root of *peccatum mortale* – mortal sin). One can find few circumstances to excuse this form of egoism: it is neither a result of natural egocentric tendencies (as cognitively based egoism is) nor a result of natural instinctive drives (as instinct-based egoism is), but a result of *hybris*, which is a malign, pathological product of human freedom.

Four additional comments are in order here.

First, since instinct-based egoism is not based on a wrongful feeling of superiority over other people, it is less morally reprehensible than *hybris*-based egoism, and since it is a result of the overabundance of instinctive drives (and the concomitant 'enslavement' to the pursuance of pleasure) which seem to be harder to control and overcome than egocentric proclivities, it also seems less morally reprehensible than cognitively based egoism.

Second, it is not clear whether the three varieties of egoism can be displayed at the same time in an agent's egoistic behaviour. Arguably, *hybris*-based egoism presupposes that other human beings are as real as oneself, so it cannot go in tandem with cognitively based egoism. Obviously, one person may manifest different forms of egoism at different times.

Third, egoism, if it is not unrestrained, seems to be biologically adaptive. It is generally in the interests of our 'genes' to place higher value on our own interests than on those of other people (unless these other people are our kin, with whom we share – to an extent which depends on the level of biological relatedness – our 'biological' interests). But, arguably, not all varieties of egoism are biologically adaptive. Egocentric cognitive biases appear to be biologically adaptive, since overestimation of the level of the reality of one's own person seems on the whole to increase our biological fitness. Similarly, strongly developed instincts of self-preservation and reproduction seem to be fitness-enhancing. However, it is dubious whether *hybris* or *superbia* – the belief in one's superiority over other persons and the resulting desire to subordinate other persons – is biologically adaptive; as will be argued in more detail in Chapter 2, it can be surmised that people who exhibited such tendencies were removed from ancestral communities, and their genes could not have been preserved in the gene pool. Therefore those who manifest *hybris* or *superbia* behave *below* their evolutionary nature.

Fourth, Adam Smith examined the question of whether people want to be moral or only want to be regarded as moral – or, in Smith's terms, whether they exhibit love or praiseworthiness, or only love of praise. Adherents of the theory of psychological egoists, such as La Rochefoucauld, denied that people have a true love of virtue; in these thinkers' view, people want only to conceal their vices and to pass for virtuous. Adam Smith disagreed, saying: 'Some splenetic philosophers, in judging human nature, have done as perverted individuals are apt to do in judging of the conduct of one another, and have imputed to the love of praise, or to what they call vanity, every action which ought to be ascribed to that of praiseworthiness' (Smith 2007: 159). Smith's view seems to be more consistent with our common experience and is assuredly not falsified by evolutionary theory: there is nothing in evolutionary theory which would forbid us to assume that human beings may be motivated by a desire for being worthy of moral praise and approval. Our egoism is just one of many motives we may have, not the only or even the dominant one.

2.2 Envy

The term 'envy' is ambiguous and can be applied to three quite distinct phenomena. What can be said about envy in general, with respect to its three forms, is that: (1) it is a three-place relation which embraces a subject (an envier), a rival (a party who is envied) and a good that the rival possesses and the envier does not (cf. D'Arms 2008); (2) it is a manifestation of the human tendency to evaluate one's own situation in a comparative way, that is, by referring it to the situation of other people; accordingly, it attests to the fact that people are concerned not with their absolute level of goods but with the relative level (that is, compared with the standing of others). We are social beings, and our sociality manifests itself, among other things, in the tendency to compare ourselves with other people, to be concerned with our 'social self' – with how we are perceived by other people. If it had not been for this tendency, envy could not appear, though, arguably, this tendency is only a necessary, not a sufficient, condition of the appearance of this emotion.

I shall now present three basic forms of envy, viz. the malicious, the just and the benign (admiring).

Malicious envy contains two elements: (1) an unpleasant emotion (distress, pain, nuisance, and so on) felt by the subject at the thought that she does not possess the good and the rival does; (2) a desire that the rival lose the good – a desire which appears despite the fact that, in the envier's view, it is not unjust that the rival possesses the good. Malicious envy may take active or passive forms: it may move an agent to take steps leading to the envied person's deprivation of the good she possesses (active envy), or it may consist in passively counting on the envied person losing the good and, if she does lose the good, in rejoicing at this fact (passive malicious envy, *Schadenfreude*). The good may be of various kinds, such as personal qualities, social position, or material goods (one may add, *en passant*, that it is rather puzzling that human beings seldom envy other people their moral qualities, the *only* qualities which are really enviable). It seems to be most destructive in the case of personal qualities (it is then called 'existential'; cf. de la Mora 1987: 69), as here it is most difficult to overcome. It should be stressed that the object of envy need not always be the good *itself*; it may also be happiness or satisfaction that the good elicits in the rival. Furthermore, the malicious envy may take two slightly different forms, depending on whether the envier *above all* wants to achieve the good the other person (the rival) possesses (and only secondarily – if she cannot achieve this good – wants the rival to lose this good), or whether she *above all* wants to 'level down' the envied person, to see her deprived of the envied good, and only secondarily wants to achieve this good. It seems that malicious envy is especially wrongful in that second case. It may be illuminating to connect the above considerations about malicious envy with the analysis of human desire proposed by the French historian and anthropologist René Girard. He has argued that the structure of human desire always has three elements: it consists of the subject (of the desire), the object, and the mediator (rival), that is, the person imitated by the subject (Girard

1961). Accordingly, our desires always have a mimetic character: we desire something because the mediator (who may also be imagined, even supernatural) – whom we admire and wish to imitate – desires it. Thus, in every instance of envy, as Girard claims, there occurs an envier's fascination for the rival/mediator. It is a 'romantic lie' (*mensonge romantique*), so Girard's argument goes, that our desires can be autonomous, authentic, genuine, spontaneous, truly 'ours'. In reality we do not choose what we really want but what the other wants (Girard applies this analysis also to the emotion of love, claiming that love always has a mediator: we love a given person because someone else – the mediator/rival – loves this person as well). One may therefore say that on Girard's view (though Girard does not put it this way), behind our desire for an object there stands an existential envy directed towards the mediator, that is, a deeper (second-order) desire to be like the mediator, to 'take over' his or her being. It is therefore a mistake to claim that the object of envy precedes the rival: it is the rival (mediator), towards whom we feel existential envy, who precedes our desire for a concrete object. Girard seems to maintain that each (first-order) desire has the mimetic character, that is, that existential envy is the omnipresent and in fact the only form of envy. This is a radical and rather counterintuitive claim. But, assuredly, many people predominantly have the kind of desires – that is, mimetic ones – which Girard so insightfully examined.

Just envy contains two elements: (1) an unpleasant emotion (distress, pain, nuisance, and so on) felt by the subject at the thought that she does not possess the good and the rival does; (2) a desire that the rival lose the good – a desire which appears because, in the envier's view, it is unjust that the rival possesses this good. Due to component (2), just envy can be considered as a primitive form of a sense of justice. This kind of envy has positive effects: it may lead to engaging in fair competition; it may sensitize an agent to various manifestations of injustice. The distinction between just and malicious envy can be traced back to Hippias of Elis, who 'distinguished two types of envy, the just one, or the envy toward undeserving people when they receive honours, and the unjust one of those who envy good people' (de la Mora 1987: 4).

Benign envy is simply an unpleasant emotion (distress, pain, nuisance, and so on) felt by the subject at the thought that she does not possess the good and the rival does, and unaccompanied by any kind of desire that the rival lose this good. As D'Arms (2008) points out, benign envy is difficult to distinguish from a positive desire for a good, that is, from greed, or from admiration for the rival. It often motivates an agent to aspire to achieve, by just means (in a process of fair competition), the envied good.

Different types of envy seem to have different sources. Luis de Granada, the sixteenth-century Spanish mystic, argued in his book *Guía de pecadores* that 'the root of envy is pride, for pride cannot suffer the superior nor the equal' (quoted in de la Mora 1987: 52). This seems to be fully apt with regard to malicious envy. The malicious envier often seems to be concerned not so much with the good the envied person possesses, but rather with gaining superiority over the rival: his main problem is often his inability to bear the fact that his situation is inferior to that of the rival, not the mere lack of the good that the rival possesses. This desire for superiority may often flow ultimately from the feeling of existential inferiority, which the envier wants to hide from himself and others. Apart from pride and an inferiority complex, one could surmise that malicious envy may also flow from 'the will to power', or from unhappiness (which makes it hard to bear the happiness or the imagined happiness of the other person), or, as claimed by the great twentieth-century Spanish philosopher Miguel de Unamuno in his book *La envidia hispánica*, from 'spiritual idleness … mental shallowness and the lack of great intimate projects' (quoted in de la Mora 1987: 56). These sources may also play a part in the two other types of envy, but assuredly assume a weaker form there.

It is worth noticing that envy is most acutely felt towards people who are in some way similar to us – in whose place we could find ourselves; who are in our proximity. However, one can imagine a kind of *acute* malicious envy, which is felt even if 'there is no relation of similarity between the envied and the envier' (de la Mora 1987: 54). Another acute form of malicious envy is *ressentiment* – a combination of malicious envy and a sense of one's own impotence – which leads, as was perspicaciously described by Scheler (who was developing Nietzsche's insights from his *Zur Genealogie der Moral*), to the distortion of the values in question: the person who feels *ressentiment* will be inclined to undermine the values which she, due to weakness, cannot achieve. The result will be an inversion of values. Paradoxically, this may cause the disappearance of envy, for 'how can one be more happy if he possesses a counter-value? He must be a poor soul, worthy of compassion and scorn' (de la Mora 1987: 69).

Finally, let me raise the question of whether envy could have been preserved by natural selection. It may be the case that some forms of envy are the product of natural selection and some others are not. It is most difficult to justify the adaptive character of malicious envy, which is one of the greatest pathologies of the human spirit. It is not only ignoble and vicious to feel (which, of course, would not by itself imply that its existence is not probable in the light of evolutionary theory), but also does not seem to bring any evolutionary advantage, as it is a highly self-destructive emotion. It decreases the envier's subjective welfare in a twofold manner: (1) malicious envy is an unpleasant vice – the envious person derives no satisfaction from envying the other person (the feeling of unpleasantness is a component of all forms of envy but it is incomparably stronger in malicious envy than in the two other forms of envy); (2) since it is radically antisocial, destroying all sympathetic connections between human beings, nobody wants to confess to possessing this vice – it generates shame and contempt. This reluctance to confess to malicious envy may also result from the fact that malicious envy is often the result of an inferiority complex. Confessing to envy would therefore amount to confessing that one feels inferior, that one's spirit is shrunken, mean, petty. This is the reason why malicious enviers so often engage in self-deception, trying to convince themselves that the emotion they feel is not malicious envy but, for instance, just envy or moral indignation. Malicious envy may also motivate the envier to take actions that will turn out to his disadvantage.

The above remarks are intended to show that it is highly improbable that malicious envy, given its self-destructive aspects, could have been preserved by natural selection. But they assume that malicious envy, as a pathology of human spirit, is quite frequent. The other argument for the nonadaptive character of malicious envy goes in a different direction: it assumes that malicious envy does not exist or exists much more rarely than is commonly supposed, and that what we consider as malicious envy usually turns out to be, on closer inspection, some other psychological phenomenon, such as just envy or moral indignation. Thus, our commonsensical picture (one shared by some philosophers, such as Arthur Schopenhauer) of human beings as frequently moved by malicious envy may be too dark; as Lars Svendsen put it, 'I trust that *Schadenfreude* is usually motivated by the feeling that suffering has been earned because the person did something evil' (Svendsen 2011: 104). Human beings may therefore exhibit a tendency to rejoice at other people's justified suffering, but not to rejoice at their unjustified suffering. This does not mean, of course, that there do not exist people who feel malicious envy, but they seem to be a negligible minority: 'hardly anyone', Svendsen claims, 'would enjoy seeing an innocent person executed' (Svendsen 2011: 104). This low frequency of occurrence of malicious envy would therefore be another argument in favour of the claim that it is not a tendency shaped by natural selection. To summarize – malicious envy is not a biological adaptation because: (*first line of argumentation*) even though it is quite frequent, it is too self-destructive to have been preserved by natural selection (it is therefore a pathology of human spirit, though a *frequent* pathology); (*second line of argumentation*) it is a very rare phenomenon (so the explanation why it could not have been preserved by natural selection is, so to say, redundant). It seems that the types of envy that are part of our nature are just envy and benign envy. Unlike malicious envy, these two types of envy seem to bring evolutionary advantages. The evolutionary benefits of benign envy are obvious: it provides a powerful motive for an agent to pursue his cherished goals. Just envy, in turn, is a manifestation of the subject's unwillingness to accept injustice and thereby a signal to the other members of a society that the agent will not accept, for instance, distributions that fail to award her a reasonable part of a good being divided. Thus, just envy strengthens the subject's motivation to pursue the good she desires and constitutes a protection against others' attempts to take advantage of her.

2.3 Aggression

One can distinguish two general types of theory of aggression. One type assumes that aggression is not a product of biological evolution but of cultural or environmental factors. This type need not detain us further, as it is based on the entirely implausible denial of the role of natural selection in shaping our psychological/behavioural propensities. The other type assumes that our propensity for aggression constitutes a product of biological evolution, and thereby is 'built into' the human genotype. There are two basic variants of this view, which can be called 'pessimistic' and '(moderately) optimistic'. The pessimistic variant assumes that aggression is an innate instinct whose energy 'accumulates' and which has to manifest itself irrespective of whether such manifestation serves any adaptive goals or is simply destructive. This view was defended by Sigmund Freud (1995) and Konrad Lorenz (1996), for example. This theory of aggression is sometimes called 'hydraulic' because it implies that aggression is like water incessantly gathering in a tank: if its pressure reaches a certain level, it will overflow. There are two important implications of this account: first, that aggression does not have only a reactive, instrumental character – it may also be nonreactive, noninstrumental, spontaneous; second, that by claiming that aggression may be purposeless, it admits the existence of absolute evil, that is, of pursuing evil not as a means to an end but as an end in itself. Which of these two variants is supported by evolutionary theory? Arguably, aggression was for our ancestors an indispensable mechanism for survival and reproduction, which enabled them to solve concrete adaptive problems in their environments (such as defending one's own life and the lives of one's family against attack, protecting property, striving for social status, discouraging sexual partners from infidelity). It was therefore reactive and instrumental rather than spontaneous and noninstrumental. Furthermore, it was not a single instinct but rather a group of distinct mechanisms which were preserved by natural selection to promote our genes. One can therefore say that the fact we have a propensity for aggression, that is, that we are not 'born pacifists', supports in some way the thesis that we are not genuinely moral, and the fact that our aggression is reactive supports in some way the thesis that we are not immoral. This account fits the picture of human nature as doubly ambivalent. Of course, there are some people who manifest pathological aggression – serving no practical purpose, directed against people who did them no wrong – but they are not numerous: they cannot be taken as typical exemplars of human nature.

One more point needs to be made. Irrespective of which theory of aggression we accept, we should be careful not to treat aggression as a key to understanding and explaining human evil. It is seldom a free-standing motive of evildoing; in point of fact, it can be such a motive only if it is understood in accordance with a noninstrumental – 'hydraulic' – theory of aggression (which is the least plausible of all theories of aggression). It is usually a part of a larger motivational structure (including, for example, various negative emotions). Furthermore, a motivational structure of evildoing does not have to contain aggression. Thus, it is hard to disagree with Mary Midgley that 'there are plenty of other ways of going wrong besides the aggressive way. To speak of all injustice as aggression seems to be a distortion of words caused by a mistaken attempt to narrow the problems of evil' (Midgley 1997: 75).

2.4 Self-Deception

The evolutionary theory teaches us that the human mind has not been designed to seek the truth as an end in itself, but only in so far as it helps to solve adaptive problems. As Michael T. Ghiselin put it:

> We are anything but a mechanism set up to perceive the truth for its own sake. Rather, we have evolved a nervous system that acts in the interests of our gonads ... If fools are more prolific than wise men, then to that degree folly will be favored by selection. (Ghiselin 1974: 1)

This statement is excessively radical and provocative, because it may suggest that the human mind is not capable of freeing itself from the fetters of evolutionary interests. But it is plausible to maintain that disinterested respect for the truth is not our natural tendency; we have to counteract our natural proclivities to reach this lofty attitude. Since the human mind is not a disinterested truthseeker, one can expect that it will be prone to generate various illusions, if this is the best way to solve a concrete adaptive problem. For instance, a well-established fact is that we are prone to self-deception, that is, to unconsciously concealing unpalatable information from ourselves and thereby distorting our picture of reality. As Michele K. Surbey put it:

> The self-deceptive mechanisms have potentially arisen as the outcome of a number of selective forces: natural selection for cognitive efficiency, maintenance of a positive outlook and hope in adversity, concealment of threatening thoughts that could limit adaptive responding, the ability to form mutually beneficial social alliances; kin selection for smooth family relationships; and sexual selection for success in mate selection and retention ... At moderate levels, self-deception promotes mental health and effective coping with environmental demands. At extremely low or high levels, individual or collective self-deception may have detrimental consequences. (Surbey 2004: 140)

Thus, self-deception, if it is at a moderate level, brings advantages, which is why it could have been preserved by natural selection. However, its dominant functions are morally negative. These functions may be offensive or defensive. As to the offensive ones, self-deception facilitates deception: an agent can more easily deceive other persons if he can deceive himself as to his real intentions; if he believes them to be morally pure, and thereby shows no signs of anxiety, his deception becomes harder to detect. As was noticed by Mark Twain in the first volume of his *Autobiography*, 'when a person cannot deceive himself, the chances are against his being able to deceive other people'. If this is true, then Robert Trivers may be right in saying that

> until shown otherwise, we should assume that the intellectually gifted are often especially prone to deception and self-deception. Those who take pride in their alleged intellectual gifts or of their particular grasp might well contemplate whether they are also more regular liars and self-deceptors. They are expected to be better at it. (Trivers 2011: 91)

As for its defensive functions, since self-deception blocks the activity of an agent's conscience, it helps him preserve a positive image of himself in spite of evidence to the contrary. As such, it is an obstacle to moral self-improvement. One can distinguish at least four morally reprehensible manifestations of self-deception connected to serving the defence of positive moral self-image. First is pharisaism, that is, self-righteous conviction about one's moral superiority over other persons, which may lead to rash moral judgements about other people – ascribing them evil intentions, interpreting their wrong behaviours as an effect of their supposedly evil character rather than of situational factors, and so on. Second is the so-called 'moralization gap', which is a partial, distorted perception of situations in which an agent is a victim or a perpetrator of an immoral act: in the former case an agent exaggerates the harm suffered; in the latter he belittles the harm done to another person. Third is hypocrisy, which may manifest in three different ways: in using different moral measures (respectively, more and less strict) in the evaluation of the other person's and one's own behaviour; in situations not clearly regulated by morality in choosing such actions which bring us benefits; and in situations clearly regulated by morality in justifying one's immoral action by saying that other people are morally even worse (the last two elements of hypocrisy were insightfully examined by Joseph Butler in *Sermon X* from his *Fifteen Sermons Preached at the Rolls Chapel*). Fourth is suspending or switching off our empathy: it is impossible to do harm to innocent persons without engaging in self-deceitful mental processes which make one believe, for example, that the innocent person is 'really' guilty, or that the person is not a 'full' human being but is instead more like an animal (animalistic dehumanization) or a machine (mechanistic dehumanization) (cf. Livingstone Smith 2007a, 2007b).

3. NEUTRAL TENDENCIES

I shall focus on three types of morally neutral tendencies, viz. (selected) emotions, hierarchical propensities, and a desire for self-transcendence. They are morally neutral in the sense that they can be put to bad or good (moral) use. But, arguably, they are biased in a morally wrong direction. Thus, if they are left in their 'natural condition', they are more likely to generate morally undesirable results than desirable ones.

3.1 (Selected) Emotions

With few exceptions (for example, empathy or envy), emotions are morally neutral in the sense that their moral evaluation, if at all possible, will usually depend on particular circumstances. They therefore cannot be evaluated *in abstracto* – that is, as types of emotions – as morally good or bad; if such an evaluation makes sense at all with regard to them, it would be perhaps apposite to call them 'morally neutral'. For instance, grief, anger, disgust, or fear may be morally acceptable depending on their causes, their intensity, and the actions to which they lead. But even though these emotions are in themselves morally neutral, it seems that their natural condition is that of imperfection. Some examples will serve to illustrate this claim.

Excessive fear leads to cowardice, which may account for a large number of examples of evildoing. Anger, as was insightfully shown by Seneca in his treatise *De ira* (On Anger), easily gets out of control and begets reactions which are disproportionate to the cause (which is the sense of being harmed); in its excessive form it may be responsible not only for violent actions, but also for various primitive legal institutions (self-help or blood revenge) overcome only after hundreds of years of the evolution of legal systems. Disgust, in turn, is a biological adaptation which serves to protect the human body from harmful substances. This kind of disgust is called 'primary'. However, it can be easily extended to serve not only the protection of the human body's purity, but also the 'purity' of the human soul or person. This variety of disgust does not have to be unjustified: it seems perfectly proper with regard, for example, to sexual intercourse in public, or to incest. It is a kind of defence against treating human beings as having only an animal nature. But in the history of law and morality, such disgust tended to be extended in an entirely arbitrary way. For instance, one of the reasons why homosexuality or interracial marriage was penalized for such a long time was the psychological process that leads to (mistakenly) taking some people's 'gut reaction' of disgust to a certain type of act (for example, homosexuality or interracial sex) to be a signal of the moral impropriety of such an act. This is a special case of the process Paul Rozin (1999) called 'moralization' – the conversion of preferences into values. Moralization of disgust can be interpreted in three different ways (cf. Pizarro et al. 2011). On the first (strong) interpretation (assumed correct by Rozin himself), disgust is regarded as a moralizing emotion: 'morally neutral acts can enter the moral sphere by dint of their being perceived as disgusting' (Pizarro et al. 2011: 268); on the second, disgust is considered as a consequence of a moral judgement; on the third, it is an 'amplifier of a moral judgment', making morally wrong acts (that is, according to some independent moral rules) seem even more wrong. According to David Pizarro and his collaborators, the strong interpretation has weaker empirical support than the weaker ones. They also notice that:

> disgust cannot be sufficient for moralization to occur because there is a plethora of behaviors that are judged by most people as disgusting but not

> immoral, such as eating pig brains or picking one's nose in private. A credible defense of the claim that disgust exerts a moralizing influence would seem to require a plausible account of why it does not seem to moralize behaviors in most cases. One possibility is that disgust exerts a moralizing influence only on behaviors for which there already exist nonmoral proscriptive norms. In these cases, the pairing of disgust with (or the tendency to be disgusted by) the behavior might cause it to be 'pushed' into the moral domain … If this view is correct, one would expect moralization over time to occur only in the disgusting behaviors for which there are already conventional norms in place. (Pizarro et al. 2011: 128)

But even if one assumes one of the weaker interpretations, disgust can still be regarded as playing an important role in moral judgement – that of its entrenchment or amplification.

It should be stressed not only that the negative consequences of emotions may concern people other than the one experiencing the emotion, but also that the latter person may also suffer from the excesses of her emotions. Given this rather obvious fact, it seems surprising that in the philosophical literature devoted to personal welfare so little attention has been paid to emotions: none of the three dominant theories of welfare which provide criteria for answering the question of how well a person's life is going for that person stresses emotions as a factor relevant for generating welfare. The mentioned dominant theories are the following: *hedonic theory*, according to which wellbeing consists in the greatest balance of pleasure over pain; *desire theory*, according to which well-being consists in preference satisfaction; and *eudaimonic theory*, which provides an objective list of goods (for example, knowledge, friendship, pleasure, autonomy) supposedly necessary for wellbeing. As regards the relations between emotions and welfare, it seems that emotions, when left in their 'natural state', constitute a serious obstacle for experiencing welfare. At least three arguments speak for this claim. First, the natural state of our emotional setup seems to be disordered: we have many emotions which pull us in various directions, and thereby jeopardize our autonomy. Second, some emotions are an important source of welfare and some others are an obstacle for experiencing welfare. But even those emotions which are a source of welfare (such as love or joy) are easily transformed into emotions which reduce welfare (for example, into grief, hatred, disappointment). Third, evolutionary biology teaches us that emotions have evolved to facilitate the realization of specific tasks which have nothing to do with our happiness. Accordingly, from the standpoint of evolutionary biology, happiness is not an ultimate goal of human actions but a means to realizing a more fundamental evolutionary goal: survival and reproduction (and therefore spreading our genes). Humans are therefore not 'destined' to be happy, but rather to effectively pass on their genes to subsequent generations. They are 'designed' to experience happiness only so long as it serves evolutionary goals. This conclusion – that emotions need to be subject to 'therapy' if they are to bring about a 'positive balance' of welfare – was reached independently by many ancient thinkers, such as Plato, the Stoics, the Sceptics, the Epicureans and the Buddhists. These considerations should not be interpreted as onesidedly critical towards emotions. Emotions are, let me repeat, neutral (with some exceptions): they can be put, not only to bad uses, but also to good ones. For instance, rage (anger) seems to be an indispensable part of our moral sensitivity; as Hannah Arendt noticed:

> Rage and the violence that sometimes – not always – goes with it belongs among the 'natural' human emotions, and to cure man of them would mean nothing less than to dehumanize or emasculate him … Absence of emotions neither causes not promotes rationality. Detachment and equanimity in view of unbearable tragedy can indeed be terrifying, namely, when they are not the result of control but an evident manifestation of incomprehension. In order to respond reasonably one must first of all be moved and the opposite of emotional is not rational, whatever that may mean, but either the inability to be moved, usually a pathological phenomenon, or sentimentality, which is a perversion of feeling. Rage and violence turn irrational only when they are directed against substitutes. (Arendt 1970: 64)

Nonetheless, if one wanted to formulate a general judgement about emotions, it seems there would be justification in saying that they seem to be biased in the wrong direction and, if left in their 'natural state', constitute an obstacle to reaching a high level of personal welfare.

3.2 Hierarchical Propensities

In his analysis of primitive egalitarianism, the evolutionist Christopher Boehm (2001) convincingly argued that human beings have been endowed by natural selection with hierarchical propensities: the will to dominate and an aversion to being dominated. In Chapter 3 I present his account of how these propensities may have given rise to the primitive egalitarian structures. Here, I would like to make some more general observations about these hierarchical propensities.

First, it seems that – apart from the will to dominate, that is, the desire for power (*libido dominandi*), and an aversion to being dominated – hierarchical propensities embrace also the propensity to obey authority (the dominant individual or the dominant group). The human tendency to obey authority, just like the two other hierarchical propensities, seems to be a biological adaptation: it is highly probable that in ancestral environments it constituted an individual's fitness-enhancing disposition in situations of conflict with more dominant members of a group. If, in ancestral environments, a conflict between a relatively powerless individual and a relatively powerful agent arose, the former agent was faced with the choice between fighting with the latter (and thereby being killed or sustaining high costs of a battle) or deferring to it (and thereby recognizing its higher place in the social hierarchy, but simultaneously avoiding the costs of fighting). Clearly, in such a situation the adaptive strategy of the relatively powerless agent would be to defer to the relatively powerful agent. Even though the result of this strategy for the relatively powerless agent would be only the second-best one (the best result for him would be the unattainable domination over the relatively powerful agent), it would be better than the result of a fight with the relatively powerful agent. Accordingly, it is plausible to maintain that a deferential strategy which directs an agent to obey more dominant members of a group has evolved. This strategy is present in many species, for example in chimpanzees, which are especially sensitive to signals of social power. It is supported by such cognitive capacities as, for example, the capacity to determine the relative power of the members of a group, or the capacity to calculate the costs and benefits of getting into a conflict with a member of a group.

Second, the ethical status of the three hierarchical propensities may be different. There seems to be little controversy that aversion to being dominated and the tendency to obey authority are indeed morally neutral. The case of desire for power is much more disputable. One could plausibly argue that it should be regarded as an immoral tendency, related to *superbia* and *hybris* (and thereby giving rise to what I have called *hybris*-based egoism).

Third, it must be admitted that exact psychological relations between these three hierarchical propensities are far from clear. For instance, according to Hannah Arendt, the desire for power goes in tandem with the tendency to obey authority, and both are incompatible with the aversion to being dominated (desire for freedom). As she put it: 'The psychological truth is that the will to power and the will to submission are interconnected; a strong disinclination to obey is often accompanied by an equally strong disinclination to dominate and command' (Arendt 1970: 46). But this view is controversial. One may just as well argue that the desire for power is especially acute among those people who are especially averse to being dominated, and thereby have 'a strong disinclination to obey'.

Fourth, it should be emphasized that the claim that hierarchical propensities are part of our 'common' biological nature, that is, were shaped by natural selection, is perhaps more controversial than claims regarding other propensities interpreted in this book as a product of biological evolution. For instance, according to many scholars, not all people exhibit a tendency to obey authority, only those who have a specific – pathological – character structure, called 'sadomasochist' by Erich Fromm and 'authoritarian' by Theodor Adorno. Such people exhibit rigid adherence to conventional values, are submissive to authority figures and are contemptuous towards people lower down the social ladder. They also desire power, are fascinated by it, and admire the powerful. They tend to divide people into two broad categories: those who possess power and those who are deprived of it. Furthermore, they are aggressive towards outgroups and inimical to introspection, reflection, creativity. They exhibit a tendency towards superstition, stereotyping and projecting their own, negative, unconscious impulses onto the outer world. They also often exhibit exaggerated concern with sexuality. As was emphasized by Fromm, this kind of character structure is a symptom of a personality defect: a person with a strong self, capable of realizing her various potentialities, will not exhibit a desire for domination. It should be stressed, however, that Fromm's views need not be regarded as inconsistent with the claim that hierarchical propensities have been shaped by natural selection, and thereby are shared by most people. One may argue that people with the authoritarian – sadomasochistic – personality belong to the margins of the bell curve of the distribution of hierarchical propensities: while most possess these propensities to some degree, people with this personality type exhibit them much more.

3.3 Desire for Self-Transcendence

The distinction between self-assertive and self-transcending tendencies was introduced by the renowned writer and philosopher Arthur Koestler in his book *The Ghost in the Machine*. Self-assertive tendencies are connected with the competition within each species for territory, mates, dominance, food (Koestler 1975: 70). They therefore serve individual, egoistic interests. Self-transcending tendencies, which are present only in human beings, are integrative: they are aimed at making an individual a part of a larger whole, and manifest themselves in 'the longing to belong' (Koestler 1975: 243). It might seem that the role of self-transcending tendencies is positive, because, as Koestler wrote, 'while the self-assertive emotions (rage, fear, anger, jealousy) narrow the field of consciousness (passion is not blind but blinkered), the self-transcending emotions expand it, until the self seems to dissolve in the "ocean feeling" of mystic contemplation or aesthetic enchantment' (Koestler 1975: 218). However, according to Koestler, self-transcending tendencies are in fact more dangerous than self-assertive ones. He claims that for most people, 'self-transcendence' is realized not in a creative way (for example, by finding an outlet in artistic or scientific activity), but by identification with a tribe, caste, nation, party, or church. It therefore takes the form of a 'regression to an infantile form of self-transcendence – immersion in the group mind is a kind of poor man's self-transcendence' (Koestler 1975: 240). Koestler made the bold (though assuredly exaggerated) claim that the main source of evil is self-transcending (integrative), not self-assertive, tendencies. What is therefore really dangerous, in his view, is the better part of human nature – its integrative/self-transcending tendencies: 'The crimes of violence committed for selfish, personal motives are historically insignificant compared to those committed *ad majorem gloriam Dei*, out of a self-sacrificing devotion to a flag, a leader, a religious faith, or a political constitution' (Koestler 1975: 234). In Koestler's view, the worst crimes of human beings 'have nothing to do with the seven deadly sins. The eighth sin, deadlier than all, self-transcendence through misplaced devotion, is not included in the list' (Koestler 1975: 236). This sin leads to the obliteration of individual egoism but also the creation of group egoism: anger, vengefulness, hate, fear do not disappear but take a different form: they are triggered by a concern not with individual interests but with group interests. The type of aggression they lead to is named by Koestler 'secondary' (as opposed to 'primary', which is caused by self-assertive tendencies). Thus, it can be said that 'the glory and the tragedy of the human condition both derive from our powers of self-transcendence' (Koestler 1975: 251).

Koestler's judgement of human beings is too harsh. For instance, he writes, in an apocalyptic tone:

> When one contemplates the streak of insanity running through human history, it appears highly probable that *homo sapiens* is a biological freak, the result of some remarkable mistake in the evolutionary process. The ancient doctrine of original sin, variants of which occur independently in the mythologies of diverse cultures, could be a reflection of man's awareness of his own inadequacy, of the intuitive hunch that something along the line of his ascent has gone wrong. (Koestler 1975: 266)

But his gloomy considerations have an undeniable value: they stress the often forgotten fact that the potential for evil inherent in our self-transcending tendencies is not to be neglected. It may be useful to put his account of the sources of evil in a broader context.

Arguably, the evil generated by self-transcending tendencies – by a desire to realize some moral ideal – is an instance of a more general category of what may be called 'moralistic evil', that is, evil justified (in the conscience of the perpetrator) by his conviction that what he is doing is morally good. In point of fact, many evil actions are regarded by their perpetrators as justified or even required by morality, especially by justice. James Gilligan's opinion is assuredly too strong but, certainly, rightly emphasizes the neglected aspect of the aetiology of crime: 'All violence is an attempt to achieve justice, or what the violent person perceives as justice … The attempt to achieve and maintain justice or to undo and prevent injustice, is the one and universal cause of violence' (Gilligan 1997: 11, 12). In similar vein: 'I have yet to see a serious act of violence that was not provoked by the experience of feeling shamed and humiliated, disrespected and ridiculed, and that did not represent the attempt to prevent or undo this "loss of face"' (Gilligan 1997: 110). The appeals to justice may therefore take place not only at the abstract level (of which Koestler writes) – that is, the level of fighting for the wellbeing of one's own group or some abstract ideal – but also at the level of individual relationships, when, for instance, a victim's kin frankly believe that justice requires them to make a bloody revenge, or when a perpetrator commits an evil act to overcome shame caused by lack of self-esteem as a result of being humiliated and treated as inferior, and not uncommonly rooted in abuse experienced as a child (cf. Gilligan 1997: 42–7). That moralistic evil is more widespread than is usually supposed seems to be confirmed by research showing that 'harmdoer guilt was higher following accidental as opposed to intentional transgression' (McGraw 1987: 247). The fact that premeditated evil elicits weaker feelings of guilt can be most plausibly interpreted by assuming that before the evildoer performed his action, he justified it morally before his conscience. Too much (superficially understood) morality may therefore have tragic consequences. According to Lars Svendsen, 'an overwhelming amount of the evil in the world happens because of love – love of self, love of family and friends, love of country, love of our abstract ideal, love of a leader' (Svendsen 2011: 124). Of course, one should be sceptical of general claims such as Gilligan's that 'all' violence is a desperate way to compensate for one's lack of self-esteem (and originally for a feeling of being humiliated or not being loved), or that the 'overwhelming amount' of evildoing is a result of excessive love. There are, of course, many other psychological sources of evildoing, such as *hybris* leading to a specific form of egoism, other forms of egoism, envy, and so on. But it cannot be doubted that moralistic evil, as Gilligan and

Svendsen rightly point out, is a much more common phenomenon than is usually supposed.

4. MORAL TENDENCIES: EVOLUTIONARY ETHICS

There is no doubt that the tendencies analysed in this section are positive from a moral point of view. However, the 'natural' (that is, shaped by natural selection) form they take is imperfect, diverging from the requirements of genuine ethics. What they give rise to is evolutionary ethics – a rudimentary, imperfect form of ethics, composed of four elements: empathy, kin altruism, tribalism, and reciprocal altruism. The term 'evolutionary ethics' is used here, as before, in a twofold sense: with reference to both the psychological, moral tendencies, and to moral rules which are 'correlates' of these tendencies.

4.1 Empathy

One should be sceptical as to the quality of our empathy in its 'primitive' form, that is, as a product of biological evolution and undeveloped by reflection and moral exercise. In order to justify this thought, I shall distinguish three types of empathy – the perfect, the truncated and the contaminated – and shall argue that the 'primitive' form of empathy is either truncated or contaminated. I shall start with a description of the type of empathy which is part of 'genuine ethics'.

Perfect empathy is the combination of three elements: cognitive empathy, affective empathy and the tendency to take empathic actions. Cognitive empathy, in its full-fledged form, is the capacity for a comprehensive and ethically proper understanding of other people's emotions. It should be stressed that cognitive empathy may, in particular cases, be confined to understanding the reasons for the other person's emotions, not the emotions themselves, since the reasons for a given emotion may fail to generate the emotion itself. To give an example: a person who has suffered the loss of reason 'laughs and sings perhaps, and is altogether insensible of his misery' (Smith 2007: 13), but the proper reaction to the loss of reason would be sorrow. An important fact about cognitive empathy is that it becomes ethically valuable only when it is coupled with affective empathy. Affective empathy, in its full-fledged form, is the tendency to emotionally respond to other people's emotions *in an ethically proper way*, which means that it implies cognitive empathy. Cognitive empathy is sometimes called 'empathy' *tout court*, while affective empathy is called 'sympathy'; the former is 'feeling someone's pain' (or pleasure), the latter 'feeling *for* someone who is in pain' or rejoicing with someone who is joyous (cf. Slote 2007: 13). The above – full-fledged – forms of cognitive and affective empathy should be distinguished from their simple forms, meaning only, respectively, an understanding of the other person's emotions, and responding to these emotions with similar emotions (sorrow to sorrow, joy to joy). The empathic action tendency is the tendency to undertake an ethically proper action (for example, helping or consoling) as a result of the emotional response to another person's emotions. The phrase 'ethically proper', which occurs in the above definitions of the constituent parts of perfect empathy, implies that *perfect empathy is not a freestanding ethical capacity*. An understanding of the other person's emotion is only partial, and may be distorted if it does not include knowledge of the causes of the emotion. For instance, the sorrow of the agent who experiences this emotion because of the loss of the beloved person is essentially different from the sorrow of an agent who experiences it because of the success of his or her enemy. One can therefore speak about a true understanding of the other person's emotion only if one knows its causes and, additionally, is capable of distinguishing between the justifying causes (that is, the reasons) and the nonjustifying causes of a given emotion. As was mentioned earlier, understanding may be confined only to the reasons for a (potential) emotion of the person with whom we empathize if that person, being unaware of these reasons, does not experience the emotion itself. Affective empathy, in turn, will be ethically proper if it means responding with sorrow to another person's justified sorrow, with joy to another person's justified joy, and with indifference or sorrow to another person's unjustified sorrow or unjustified joy (the sorrow of the empathic person would not be caused in this case by the other person's emotion as such, but rather by the fact that the other person reacts in a morally inadequate way). One should also add that affective empathy need not be a response to an emotion: it may be a response only to the other person's reasons for a (potential) emotion – reasons of which she may be unaware (for instance, we empathize with a person who has lost a close relative but is not yet aware of that loss and so does not yet feel sorrow). It is clear that perfect empathy is not necessary for moral action: one can easily imagine a nonempathic agent strictly following moral rules and thereby undertaking moral actions. But it must be admitted that perfect empathy provides an especially strong motivation to undertake moral actions. Furthermore, if one were to provide an agent-based, not action-based, moral evaluation of agents undertaking moral actions, then the evaluation of a perfectly empathic agent would undoubtedly be higher than that of an unwavering but nonempathic follower of moral rules. One may notice in passing that it follows from the above analysis that the ethics of *perfect* empathy might arguably be a plausible ethics, but it would not be a pure ethics of empathy, because the very concept of perfect empathy, as defined in this chapter, is a normative one – that is, it implies a set of moral rules prescribing when, in what circumstances, and towards whom empathy is demanded; what actions should be taken as a result of the empathic response to the other person's feelings; and how to decide conflicts of empathic impulses. That an ethics of empathy cannot be built was the thesis held also by Max Scheler (1980: 234–53), who stressed that for empathy (or sympathy, the term he used) to have ethical value, it must be empathy with emotions *deserving* empathy, and in order to distinguish the emotions deserving empathy from those undeserving of it we must have prior (independent of empathy itself) conceptions of justice, blame, responsibility.

Truncated empathy lacks one of the free elements of perfect empathy, or contains one or more of them but only in a truncated form. Truncated empathy may therefore take various forms, ranging from those which are morally reprehensible to those which are morally commendable. The morally reprehensible form of truncated empathy is the combination of cognitive empathy with the absence of affective empathy, that is, the combination of a capacity to recognize the other person's emotions with an incapacity to react to them. This kind of combination is characteristic for psychopaths, though, arguably, is not sufficient for creating a psychopathic personality. As Simon Baron-Cohen (2011: 154) noted, the psychopath, apart from displaying this combination, must additionally be 'morally negative'. This implies that the combination of cognitive empathy with the absence of affective empathy is, by itself, not sufficient for generating a psychopathic personality; for this personality to arise, some kind of profound indifference to moral rules or to other people's wellbeing is needed. This indifference to other persons can be described in terms proposed by Martin Buber (2012): as the tendency to treat other persons as things, or to replace the personal relation based on '*You*' with the impersonal relation based on '*It*' (of course, this is still not an explanation of this tendency, but simply highlights its different aspect). The morally commendable form of truncated empathy consists of cognitive empathy and affective empathy in their simple forms (that is, not supported by moral rules). Clearly, this combination is desirable: a person who displays these two forms of empathy exhibits sensitivity to the other person's feelings, and this sensitivity is valuable in itself. But, as mentioned above, this kind of sensitivity, if unsupported by the knowledge of moral rules and the motivation to analyse the causes of the other person's emotions, is likely to lead to morally improper actions if the other person's emotions are unjustified (if, for example, the person empathized with feels sorrow for immoral reasons).

Contaminated empathy arises by admixing one of the following four amoral or nonmoral elements to perfect empathy, viz. (1) *a feeling of relief*, that is, thankfulness at the contrast between our good fortune and the sufferer's misfortune; (2) *a feeling of anxiety* about our own good fortune arising at the sight of the sufferer's misfortune; (3) *a feeling of superiority* over the other person (*pity*); and (4) *personal distress*: the unpleasant feeling that arises at the sight of the sufferer's sorrow, caused by the image of suffering rather than by anxiety about one's own good fortune.

It is to be emphasized that all four motives contaminating perfect empathy are self-regarding – they have as their ultimate end the well-being of the agent, not the interests of the other person. They can also function as freestanding motives, in which case they can be regarded as various forms of what may be called *pseudoempathy*. The first two of these motives were analysed by Samuel Butler in *Fifteen Sermons Preached at the Rolls Chapel*, in his famous polemics using Hobbes's definition of pity as 'fear felt for oneself at the sight of another's distress'. This was nicely summarized by Charlie Dunbar Broad in the following passage:

> He [Butler] points out (a) that, on this definition, a sympathetic man is *ipso facto* a man who is nervous about his own safety, and the more sympathetic he is the more cowardly he will be. This is obviously contrary to fact. (b) We admire people for being sympathetic to distress; we have not the least tendency to admire them for being nervously anxious about their own safety. If Hobbes were right admiration for sympathy would involve admiration for timidity. (c) Hobbes mentions the fact that we tend specially to sympathise with the troubles of our friends, and he tries to account for it. But, on Hobbes's definition, this would mean that we feel particularly nervous for ourselves when we see a friend in distress. Now, in the first place, it may be doubted whether we do feel any more nervous for ourselves when we see a friend in distress than when we see a stranger in the same situation. On the other hand, it is quite certain that we do feel more sympathy for the distress of a friend than for that of a stranger. Hence it is impossible that sympathy can be what Hobbes says that it is. Butler himself holds that when we see a man in distress our state of mind may be a mixture of three states. One is genuine sympathy, i.e., a direct impulse to relieve his pain. Another is thankfulness at the contrast between our good fortune and his ill luck. A third is the feeling of anxiety about our own future described by Hobbes. These three may be present in varying proportions, and some of them may be wholly absent in a particular case. But it is only the first that any plain man means by 'sympathy' or 'pity'. (Broad 1930, p. 53)

At the end of this passage Broad treats 'sympathy' (or compassion) and 'pity' as identical. But there are good reasons to treat them as distinct. The distinction was neatly made by Philip Mercer (1972: 18) and recalled by David E. Cartwright (1988). Compassion, corresponding to what I have called 'perfect empathy', is an altruistic – *other-regarding* – virtue having as its ultimate aim the wellbeing of the other person. Pity, by contrast, is egoistic, or *self-regarding*: it is expressive of contempt towards the other person and aims at heightening one's self-esteem and feeling of power. It embraces cognitive empathy but it lacks affective empathy: there is no feeling of sorrow at the other person's suffering or, at best, the feeling of sorrow is mixed with joy at the possibility of increasing one's self-esteem and the feeling of one's own power. Cartwright characterizes it in the following way:

> the pitier is superior in status to the pitied. We do not pity those we respect or those we judge superior to ourselves – unless we wish to level them by devaluing their status ... By pitying them, I elevate myself. I boost my feelings of self-esteem by exercising my pity. The same is true when I pity someone who is suffering ... The sufferer is helped, but helped in order to enhance my feelings of superiority. In these regards, pity is self-regarding. If we have general duties to respect others, pity incites their violations. If the moral goodness of beneficence is due to a desire to pursue another's well-being, the help rendered out of pity is not morally good. (Cartwright 1988: 559)

Pity is not morally good because it does not lead to 'acts of beneficence for the right sorts of reasons' (Cartwright 1988: 560).

Let me summarize the main conceptual distinctions introduced above:

(1) *Perfect empathy* consists of ethically grounded cognitive empathy, ethically grounded affective empathy, and the tendency to undertake morally adequate actions as a result of affective empathy.
(2) *Truncated empathy* appears if one of the elements of perfect empathy is lacking, or if at least one of its elements is not supported by the clear knowledge of moral rules (that is, it is not ethically grounded, or a tendency to undertake actions is not guided by the clear knowledge of moral rules).
(3) *Contaminated empathy* is perfect empathy combined with one of the four self-regarding motives: a feeling of relief that another, not myself, is the victim of suffering; anxiety about my own future; a feeling of superiority (pity); personal distress.
(4) *Pseudoempathy* occurs if any of the four 'contaminating' motives appears as a freestanding motive.

As mentioned above, it was the view of a number of philosophers, including Hobbes and Nietzsche, that perfect empathy does not exist; that in each empathic action one can always seek out some egoistic motive. But this view does not seem convincing: common experience, the famous experiments on the empathy–altruism hypothesis carried out by C.D. Batson (1991), and the strong philosophical arguments raised by Butler support the view that perfect empathy (characterizing a genuinely ethical person) does exist (though certainly is not a frequent phenomenon). Furthermore, as Cartwright aptly remarks (in the spirit of Butler's critique of psychological egoism defended by Hobbes),

> simply showing that an agent may derive pleasure, relieve feelings of sorrow or grief, feel self-satisfied, or better about oneself for helping another, is not to show that the action is self-regarding. In the same regard, simply arguing that in one sense all interests are mine, in the sense that I possess them, does not show that this is a self-regarding interest. What he had to show was that the end of the action was the agent's pleasure, feelings of self-esteem or superiority. (Cartwright 1988: 564)

Thus, Nietzsche could have not proved that the agent can never have the other person's wellbeing as his end. What he was able to prove was that in many cases of purported altruistic empathy, a different – egoistic – motivation may in fact be operating. But one must concede that there is some reason in Nietzsche's claim: it seems that perfect empathy rarely or never appears in an uncontaminated form. Let me repeat, however, that Nietzsche believed that perfect empathy never exists, even in a contaminated form; he believed that all forms of empathy are at bottom egoistic, that is, are forms of pseudoempathy. This is an extreme and implausible view. The plausible view, however, is that our empathy, in the form shaped by biological evolution, is *very far from being perfect.* In addition to the fact that it is imperfect, very often contaminated by various forms of pseudoempathy, it has three other defects.

First, its 'natural', that is, evolutionary-shaped level of intensity, is not very high. To put it more precisely, this feature (intensity of empathy), as most other features, has a bell-curve distribution over the entire population, and the level of empathy which is exhibited by most people does not seem to be very high. The evolutionary reason for this fact is that people with a very high level of empathy would be unable to take sufficient care of their own interests and people with a very low level of empathy would pose a threat to a group and be eliminated; as a result, neither very high nor very low-level empathy could become dominant in the population. La Rochefoucauld was right in saying that 'nous avons tous assez de force pour supporter les maux d'autrui'.

Second, primitive empathy is partial, that is, sensitive to factors which are often ethically irrelevant. We are more likely to empathize with those who are similar to us (in various regards – for instance, in terms of physical appearance, social status, race), who are more cute, who are our kin, or who are simply more visible. Especially interesting manifestations of the last of these four types of partiality are the 'identifiable victim' effect and the 'collapse of compassion' effect. The former consists in greater willingness to help a concrete, individualized victim than a 'statistical' victim (cf. Jenni, Loewenstein 1997). The latter (which can be interpreted as a partial explanation of the former) consists in decreased empathy as the number of victims increases (Slovic 2007). Such a decrease may take one of two forms – either less or more radical. In the less radical form, empathy is assumed to be subject to the law which is analogous to the law of decreasing marginal utility: successive victims elicit smaller 'marginal' increases of empathy (or, alternatively, the value – utility – assigned to each successive human life is smaller). This means that the 'total empathy' (that is, empathy for the entire group of victims) increases disproportionately slowly with an increasing number of victims. In the more radical form, an increasing number of victims causes a decrease in 'total empathy'. It is hard to say which of the two versions of the effect really occurs. Slovic thinks it is the more radical. But even if it is the less so, it still illustrates the limitations of our empathy, or, as Slovic puts it more strongly and aptly, 'a fundamental deficiency in our humanity' (Slovic 2007: 79). The limitation is in fact an illustration of the priority we give to our own interest over the interest of others: our small loss moves us much more strongly than other people's great loss. As Adam Smith memorably wrote:

> Let us suppose that the great empire of China, with all its myriads of inhabitants, was suddenly swallowed up by an earthquake, and let us consider how a man of humanity in Europe, who had no sort of connexion with that part of the world, would be affected upon receiving intelligence of this dreadful calamity. He would, I imagine, first of all, express very strongly his sorrow for the misfortune of that unhappy people, he would make many melancholy reflections upon the precariousness of human life, and the vanity of all the labours of man, which could be annihilated in a moment. He would too, perhaps, if he was a man of speculation, enter into many reasonings concerning the effects which this disaster might produce upon the commerce of Europe, and the trade and business of the world in general. And when all his fine philosophy was over, when all these humane sentiments had been fairly expressed, he would pursue his business or his pleasure, take his repose or his diversion, with the same ease of tranquility, as if no such accident had happened. The most frivolous disaster which could befall himself would occasion a more real disturbance. If he was to lose his little finger tomorrow,

> he would not sleep tonight; but provided he never saw them, he will snore with the most profound security over the ruin of a hundred millions of his brethren, and the destruction of that immense multitude seems plainly an object less interesting to him, than this paltry misfortune of his own. (Smith 2007: 136–7)

It is important not to interpret these facts onesidedly, treating them as illustrating the darkness of the human heart. One can present them in a less pessimistic light. For instance, one may argue that the phenomenon of 'the collapse of compassion' simply shows that our empathy 'evolved to protect individuals and their small family and community groups from great, visible, immediate danger; this effective system did not evolve to help us respond to distant, mass murder' (Slovic 2007: 87). Or one may say it is a rational response of human agents observing a tragedy of a large group: they 'expect the needs of large groups to be potentially overwhelming, and, as a result, they engage in emotion regulation to prevent themselves from experiencing overwhelming levels of emotion' (Cameron, Payne 2011: 14). However, even granting that our defective empathy may be understandable and perhaps even justified, we can still maintain that this kind of empathy is far from being ethically proper.

Third, our 'natural' empathy is unreliable – it can be rather easily suspended or weakened. Without going into an analysis of various ways in which the perpetrators of great atrocities 'switched off' their empathic reaction (for example, by dehumanizing the victims), let me mention less dramatic examples from our everyday experience. Most of us know all too well that the strength of our empathy depends on such morally irrelevant factors as whether we are tired or in a rush; we also know how easily empathy can be overshadowed by strong emotions (not only negative, such as anger, envy, hatred, or a desire for revenge; positive emotions of happiness may also engender a high level of self-centredness). As was mentioned in Section 2.4 of this chapter, suspension of empathy does not seem possible without the mechanisms of self-deception.

Having reached the end of my analysis of empathy, I would like to make two additional observations.

The first concerns the definitional relations between evil and empathy. Simon Baron-Cohen (2011) defined evil as an erosion of empathy. This definition is inadequate for two reasons. Since it is focused on the internal state of the perpetrator of evil, it does not make precise what concrete 'effects' in the external world must be caused by an action for it to be called 'evil'. Arguably, in order to make a proper account of evil, we must combine the account of the internal state (motivation) of the agent with the account of the action this motivation leads to. But even as an account of the evil motivation, this definition is not apt – it is too narrow. It is based on the assumption that only empathy can block our evil actions. But this is implausible. An unempathic agent may nonetheless be virtuous or obey rules. Thus, if one wanted to enumerate various possible 'brakes' on immoral behaviour, one should mention at least two additional 'mechanisms' apart from empathy, viz. virtues and rules.

The second observation concerns relations between empathy and feelings of guilt. As it turns out, they are quite strictly connected to each other. The strength of our feelings of guilt depends not only on the type of our wrongdoing (as it should) but also on the type of person whom we wronged. The feelings are stronger if we wronged a person with whom we want to keep close and positive relations; one may say that we may have sincere feelings of guilt only towards those persons with regard to whom we can be truly empathic. Consequently, the more empathic persons are, the more likely are they to be guilt-prone. It is also worth recalling Dostoyevsky's observation in his *Memoirs from the House of the Dead* that he met no criminals with feelings of guilt. This is a sadly predictable reaction: if an agent decided to commit an evil act, and thereby considered it the right thing to do, he should not be expected to feel guilty because of this act (unless he changed its moral evaluation, which occurs rarely). Guilt may also take other improper (false) forms (cf. Tournier 1962: 64–98). It may be insincere: an agent may only pretend to feel guilty. Or an agent may sincerely feel guilty, but his guilt may be irrational. The irrationality is extreme if the agent feels guilty about what, on virtually all moral theories, he cannot be blamed for: for example, for being healthy (when others are ill), for having survived a natural catastrophe, for having survived a concentration camp. It is less extreme, though still irrational, if an agent failed to perform a supererogatory action, that is, he did not decide to expose himself to a high risk in order to help a person in danger. Arguably, this broad or overly sensitive variety of the feeling of guilt is not a product of natural selection; rather, it arises as a result of specific personal experiences. But what may have been such a product is the ease with which guilt is suspended or 'silenced' – various techniques of neutralization of conscience, with which we come up spontaneously and with little effort (for instance those described by Gresham Sykes and David Matza (1957), viz. the condemnation of the condemners, the appeal to higher loyalty, the denial of injury, responsibility, or the victim) prove to be distressingly effective.

4.2. Kin Altruism

The theory of inclusive fitness, originally put forward by William D. Hamilton (1964) as a correction of the theory of natural selection, is contemporarily regarded as an integral part of the theory of natural selection. This theory states that an individual's reproductive success embraces not only her/his personal reproductive success (as was implied originally by the theory of natural selection), that is, the number of her/his offspring, but also the reproductive success of other individuals discounted by their coefficients of relatedness to the individual. The theory of inclusive fitness explains why individuals display altruistic behaviour towards their kin, that is, it partly resolves the so-called 'problem of altruism' (the existence of altruistic behaviour was a puzzle for evolutionary biologists, including Darwin himself, before the theory of inclusive fitness was propounded). To put it more precisely: the theory of inclusive fitness explains the existence of biological kin altruism, as it leads to the prediction that natural selection will favour the psychological mechanisms which make people behave altruistically towards their kin – because they bear a high percentage of their genes – and that the degree of altruism will be in inverse proportion to the degree of genetic relatedness. However, kin altruism also has a dark side. It leads to nepotism and favouritism towards kin. It may also be argued that its consequence (or, rather, a side effect) is tribalism (of which I write more in the next section). Kin altruism also seems to lie at the basis of the mechanism called 'discriminative parental solicitude' (cf. Daly, Wilson 1999: 37). This mechanism consists in a greater likelihood of adult persons delivering their finite resources to those children who are most capable of turning them into reproductive success. The existence of this mechanism accounts for the fact that children unrelated to an adult person and children related to that person but who are physically or mentally handicapped are at increased risk of abuse on the part of that person. The empirical data confirm the hypothesis that the psychological mechanisms responsible for child abuse have biological foundations. For instance, they reveal one of the consequences of 'discriminative parental solicitude', which is called 'the Cinderella effect': this is that 'the probability that a stepfather or boyfriend of the mother will kill an unweaned infant is nearly *one hundred times* greater than is the probability of death at the hands of an infant's genetic father' (Jones, Goldsmith 2005: 453). These data remain telling even if we allow for the obvious fact that the overwhelming majority of stepfathers do not kill their stepchildren and that most step-parents also manifest true concern for the children. This is arguably one of the most dramatic examples of 'secondary evil' generated by one of our moral tendencies, viz. kin altruism.

4.3 Tribalism (Group Altruism)

Tribalism consists in treating one's group as better than other groups, and consequently holding negative emotions towards the other group. It is typical of a primitive communal mentality and is aimed at ensuring the survival and prosperity of the group. It is based on the assumption that the members of one's own group and the members of other groups are different in essential aspects, which justifies undertaking sacrificial actions for the sake of the former and manifesting deep hostility towards the latter. The distinct features of tribal ethics are therefore exclusivity – the circle of people who deserve moral respect is narrowed down to the members of one's own group – and (misguided) idealism – people are expected to make great sacrifices for the sake of their own group. Darwin described these ethics in the following way:

> Actions are regarded by savages, and were probably so regarded by primeval man, as good or bad, solely as they obviously affect the welfare of the tribe – not that of the species, nor that of an individual member of the tribe. This conclusion agrees well with the belief that the so-called moral sense is aboriginally derived from the social instincts, for both relate at first exclusively to the community. The chief causes of the low morality of savages, as judged by our standard, are, firstly, the confinement of sympathy to the same tribe. Secondly, powers of reasoning insufficient to recognizing the bearing of many virtues, especially of the self-regarding virtues, on the general welfare of the tribe. Savages, for instance, fail to trace the multiplied evils consequent on a want of temperance, chastity, etc. And, thirdly, weak power of self-command; for this power has not been strengthened through long-continued, perhaps inherited habit, instruction, and religion. (Darwin 1871: 80)

There is controversy among evolutionists as to the origins of tribal thinking. There are two main arguments for the claim that tribalism is embedded in our biological predispositions, that is, that there exist biological predispositions whose correlates are the rules that constitute tribal ethics (for example, such rules as 'treat your own group as better than the other groups', 'be ready to sacrifice your own individual good for the sake of the good of the group to which you belong'; 'do not trust the members of other groups'). The first argument appeals to the theory of kin altruism, the second to the theory of group altruism. These two evolutionary explanations of the emergence of predispositions underlying tribal ethics need not be viewed as mutually exclusive: they can be regarded as complementary. Let me present these arguments in somewhat greater detail.

The first argument says that the emergence of predispositions underlying tribal ethics can be explained by the theory of kin altruism. According to this argument, therefore, tribalism would in fact be a result of an extension of the circle of the objects of ethical concern, from a very narrow circle of the closest kin to a still narrow, though slightly broader circle of the members of one's group. The extension may be interpreted in terms of mistake or side effect: we treat members of our groups as our kin because the mechanisms of distinguishing between kin and non-kin are imprecise and fallible.

The second argument states that these predispositions are the product of the mechanism of genetic group selection. The theory of genetic group selection asserts that group selection may favour the emergence of the propensity to sacrifice oneself for the sake of the group, because groups consisting of individuals endowed with this propensity are likely to fare better than and prevail over groups consisting of individuals without such propensity. This explanation assumes, then, that the propensity to undertake sacrificial acts for the sake of the group (let us call this propensity 'group altruism') may have evolved, because fitness losses incurred by individuals endowed with such a propensity are compensated by the superior performance of the group to which they belong. It is worth mentioning that some fragments from Charles Darwin's writings suggest that he was inclined to accept the idea of group selection as an explanation for the evolution of human faculties or psychological features; see, for example, his statement that 'A tribe including many members who, from possessing in a high degree the spirit of patriotism, fidelity, obedience, courage, and sympathy, were always ready to aid another, and to sacrifice themselves for the common good, would be victorious over most other tribes' (Darwin 1871: 89). However, this explanation is controversial. The basic argument advanced against it is that if an egoist appears within a group of group-altruists, he will have a higher chance of survival and reproduction than group-altruists, so that after a few generations the initially altruistic group will become dominated by egoists. This is the so-called 'subversion from within argument' against the idea of group selection, raised by proponents of the view that the basic unit of selection is gene, not group (cf. Williams 1966; Dawkins 1976). It should be noted, however, that in recent times the idea of genetic group selection has been rehabilitated to some extent. As Elliott Sober and David S. Wilson (1998) have demonstrated, should some conditions be met (and, as they argue, the satisfaction of these conditions is facilitated by cultural evolution), it is possible that between-group selection for group altruism (that is, for the propensity to sacrifice oneself for the group) will prevail over within-group selection for egoism (that is, for the propensity to exploit group-altruists). The conditions are as follows: genetic variation between groups must be greater than genetic variation within groups; the speed of between-group selection must be relatively higher than the speed of within-group selection; in order to hinder the process of within-group selection for egoism, the groups must grow, disperse, fission, and integrate in optimal times. The problem with the idea of genetic group selection is that these conditions are difficult to satisfy. For instance, the processes that uphold genetic variation between the groups and select between the groups are usually weaker than the processes that disrupt genetic variation and select within groups (for example, the processes of migrations among groups).

It is worth noticing, at the end of this section, that the question of whether human nature is primarily individualistic or social (communal) – whether, in the early stages of history, human beings had felt themselves primarily to be separate entities with their own interests, or parts of a larger whole, of a community (with their individual ego having been, so to say, not distinct) – is closely related to the question (still not answered clearly by evolutionary biologists) about the *depth* of the rootedness of tribalism in human nature. But it seems it can be reasonably assumed that tribalism is not a superficial part of human nature (and is closely related to the self-transcending tendencies discussed in Section 3.3).

4.4. Reciprocal Altruism

A precise characterization of the human tendency to engage in reciprocal altruism was provided by game theorists, who have identified the kind of behaviour (strategy) which is most effective in generating beneficial (utility-maximizing) outcomes in relations of social exchange, and thereby is likely to have been preserved by natural selection. In their view, the bulk of human beings are neither universal cooperators – 'suckers' – nor universal defectors – 'cheaters' – but rather tit-for-tat (*TFT*) players (cf. Axelrod 1984). *TFT* is strikingly simple, as it starts with a cooperative move and then imitates an opponent's last move. This strategy is therefore nice, reciprocal, (moderately) forgiving, not (maliciously) envious, and clear – that is, someone using this strategy is never first to defect, punishes defectors and therefore cannot be exploited by them, forgives after an opponent's single period of cooperation, and does not want to gain more than her opponent. Being easily recognizable, this strategy is effective in generating cooperation. The insight that, in a series of Prisoner's Dilemmas (modelling the relations of social exchange), *TFT* is the strategy that fares best and thereby has the highest chance of reproductive success in reciprocal relationships is a very intuitive one, for it accords with the commonsense observation that repeated interactions create the possibility to punish defectors and thereby discourage them from defecting.

Two additional remarks on this strategy are in order. First, *TFT* can be seen as embodying moral rules of a specific character, viz. conditional and prudential. These rules can be presented in two equivalent ways. One can say that *TFT* embodies the rule 'Do unto others as you would have them do unto you *only if* others do unto you as they would have you do unto them'; or that it embraces the following rules: (1) start by cooperating; (2) do good to those who do good to you and do harm to those who do harm to you; (3) be (moderately) forgiving; (4) do not be (maliciously) envious (cf. Singer 1995: 129–53). Thus, since *TFT* does not prescribe unconditional moral action, it cannot be regarded as embodying a moral rule *sensu stricto*; it is a prudential rule, that is, one aimed at serving our own long-term interests. Second, an interesting problem connected with the research on the *TFT* strategy concerns the role of emotions in shaping the behaviour of agents involved in the Prisoner's Dilemma-like interactions. One way in which emotions may affect the agent's behaviour is by supporting the mechanism of reciprocal altruism: certain emotions (for example, anger, guilt, gratitude, or a 'second-level' emotion – empathy) may mimic the behaviour of the *TFT* players. Furthermore, emotions can affect the agent's utility function in such a way that it changes the game in which the agent was initially involved. For instance, the game that was initially the Prisoner's Dilemma may become (say, under the influence of the emotion of empathy, which makes the agent derive disutility from her opponent's misfortune) a game in which a rational choice is cooperation rather than defection; thus, emotions may induce agents to act cooperatively even in the one-shot Prisoner's Dilemma (by transforming this game into a different one). Thus, the relations of social exchange may have created a strong selective pressure for the appearance of certain emotions: these emotions are supposed to 'move' the agents to take actions they would have taken were they able to carry out the rather complicated calculations that a fully rational player is expected to make. They therefore serve as proxies for the *TFT* strategy: agents who act on these emotions act *as if* they played the *TFT* strategy (cf. Trivers 1971).

5. EVOLUTIONARY ETHICS AND THE NECESSITY TO OVERCOME IT

Evolutionary ethics embraces ethics of empathy, family (kin altruism) ethics, tribal ethics, and reciprocal altruism ethics. This ethics, 'encoded' in our biological nature, is primitive: its level of impartiality is low, and as a result it may generate morally undesirable (from the standpoint of genuine ethics) consequences. More generally, the ambivalence of the elements of evolutionary ethics can take two forms: first, a lack of moral purity; second, undesirable side effects. Kin altruism may lead to nepotism, favouritism of kin, and discriminatory parental solicitude (and the consequent 'Cinderella effect'). Tribal ethics is based on the assumption that members of one's own group and members of other groups are different in essential aspects, which justifies undertaking moral actions for the sake of the former and manifesting hostility towards the latter (it leads therefore to ingroup cooperation and out-group competition). It cannot be regarded as a part of genuine ethics because of its exclusivity (a narrow definition of the circle of people who deserve moral respect), and thereby its arbitrariness, which leads to a double standard in moral action and moral evaluation. Reciprocal altruism (tit-for-tat) ethics cannot be regarded as embodying moral rules *sensu stricto:* its prescription of cooperation is conditional and prudential, that is, aimed at serving the agent's long-term interests, and is therefore contaminated by egoism. The ethics of empathy is also imperfect, since empathy in its natural form is fragile (easy to 'suspend'), limited (partial), often blind to morally relevant factors, and impure, that is, contaminated by various forms of pseudoempathy (the feeling of relief, the feeling of anxiety, the feeling of superiority over the other person, or personal distress). Accordingly, in order to reach full moral development, one must pass from evolutionary ethics to genuine ethics. At the level of genuine ethics one therefore abstains not only from primary evil (which is absent already on the level of evolutionary ethics) but also from secondary evil, that is, evil caused by moral (as well as neutral) tendencies shaped by natural selection.

In the considerations pursued in this chapter I have implicitly assumed that human beings are endowed with freedom of will, that is, the capacity to choose different actions in a given moment. Thus, an agent who has chosen an action at a given moment has free will if she could have chosen some other action at that moment. The capacity for freedom resides in or is strictly connected with our capacity for symbolic thinking and anticipating the consequences of our actions, which, though itself the product of natural selection, enables us, so to say, to transcend the boundaries of biology – to liberate ourselves from the force of our evolved propensities (cf. Ayala 2010). As a result, humans are not 'closed' in their individual perceptions (which can be called 'the first-level representations of the world'). Owing to their capacity to use abstract notions, they create symbolic representations of the world (which can be called 'second-level representations of the world'). This capacity (arguably unique among animals) creates, as one may call it, an ontological crevice between humans and the world, and thereby fundamentally detaches the two from each other. This is the anthropocentric (strongly humanistic) assumption that cannot be conclusively proved (and which is not popular in the contemporary climate of opinion: cf., for example, Pietrzykowski 2016). I shall confine myself to invoking three arguments in its favour. The first one says that 'our personal experience indicates that the possibility to choose between alternatives is genuine rather than only apparent' (Ayala 2010: 324); the second that 'when we confront a given situation that requires action on our part, we are able mentally to explore alternative courses of action, thereby extending the field within which we can exercise our free will' (Ayala 2010: 324). Third and furthermore, as was forcefully argued by Kant, it seems that one cannot speak meaningfully about responsibility for actions, and about (moral) evil as such, if we do not assume that human beings are free. Similar thoughts have been defended by many other philosophers. For instance, Lars Svendsen claimed that 'moral evil begins with free will, while the causes of natural evil are purely natural. Biology doesn't have the capacity to define the moral concept of evil and at most can only explain away the phenomenon' (Svendsen 2011: 21). Indeed, one cannot biologically 'define' the concept of moral evil, because biology cannot help us distinguish between good and evil and because it cannot explain the ultimate source of evil (free will). It must be added, however, that it can be immensely helpful, even indispensable, in explaining our 'gravity', that is, the psychological propensities which 'push' us towards (nonbiologically defined) evil actions (which indeed could not be called 'evil' if not finally approved or selected by our free will).

6. INSTEAD OF A SUMMARY: ON SIMILARITIES BETWEEN THE EVOLUTIONARY ACCOUNT OF EVIL AND THE CHRISTIAN AND KANTIAN ACCOUNTS

The choice of the Christian and Kantian accounts of evil as a background against which to see more clearly the doubly ambivalent view of human nature is not accidental: there are deep similarities between the evolutionary, Christian and Kantian accounts.

6.1 The Christian Account

Since Christianity gave rise to many different currents of thought, one cannot maintain that there exists one specifically Christian account of evil. I shall present two such accounts (which are dominant in the Catholic variant of Christianity): a less and a more optimistic. They share the following two assumptions: that evil has a negative character, and that evil flows from freedom. I shall have more to say about the second assumption in the Epilogue to this book. Here I shall focus on the first one, which is a basis of division between these two accounts. The thesis about the negative character of evil may be understood morally or ontologically (these two senses are to a large extent separate from each other). From the standpoint of the comparison of the evolutionary and the Christian accounts of evil, the moral sense is essential. I shall therefore make this my focus, and make only some general comments on the ontological sense.

The moral sense is expressed by the statement that our will, as St Augustine put it in *De Civitate Dei*, is not an efficient but a deficient cause of evil acts: it causes evil not because it chooses evil as such, but because it chooses an inferior good. Evil is therefore negative in the sense that it consists in *not choosing* a superior good and in choosing an *inferior* good. This claim implies that human will is, basically, directed towards goodness; as the Thomist philosopher Josef Pieper put it,

> every sin consists in longing for a passing good: in every sin there lurks the desire to have and to enjoy, which is in fact why sin can never become infinitely bad, a pure evil. Because the reality of the world is good, no human deed can ever take on the character of being definitive evil, guilt, or sin. (Pieper 2001: 57)

It is noteworthy that two interpretations of this statement are possible: a less and a more optimistic one. On the less optimistic interpretation, this statement is simply another way of saying that human beings do not commit absolute evil; that choosing evil is always choosing an inferior good. If understood in this way, it is, of course, fully compatible with the view of human nature as doubly ambivalent. One may, however, interpret it more optimistically (as the Thomist thinkers tend to do), viz.: that each of the natural human appetites, in which evil is ultimately rooted, are either moral (basically good) or morally neutral, and that thereby there do not exist natural tendencies which could be called 'immoral'. This is a controversial and *too* optimistic claim, since, as I have argued, human beings were endowed by nature with immoral tendencies. So there is full consistency between the less optimistic variant and the doubly ambivalent view of human nature, and partial consistency between the more optimistic variant and the doubly ambivalent view. However, even in the latter case, essential consistency exists, because the doubly ambivalent view assumes that none of the immoral tendencies are of such a kind as to deserve to be called 'absolutely evil'. What is more, there is also a distinct note of pessimism even in the more optimistic variant of the Christian account. Even though it asserts that our natural appetites are good, and our will directed towards goodness, it also claims (like the less optimistic variant) that the present situation of man (due to his contamination by original sin) is imperfect: it is that of, to use the Christian term, *cor curvatum in seipsum*, wherein man's heart becomes turned towards itself, he makes himself his final end, self-love is his dominant motive, and he may even commit *peccatum mortale*, or 'turning away from God' (I shall return to this problem in the Epilogue). Thus, the Christian and the evolutionary account of evil share essential points: that human nature is flawed, but not fundamentally flawed (because there does not exist absolute evil), and that as such it must be (morally) transformed.

To have a more complete picture of the Christian account of evil, two additional remarks are in order.

First, there is also a different, teleological, understanding of the moral sense of the Christian claim that *malum est privatio*, that is, that evil is negative. If we assume that human beings are supposed to realize a certain God-given purpose (*telos*) and thereby fulfil their morally understood nature, then, should an agent act in a wrongful way, he will fail to reach what he ought to reach (his *telos* as a human being). As a result of his wrongdoing, his nature suffers a *deficiency*, a *lack*; his (empirical) nature is, so to say, incomplete, since it did not live up to its task. But this understanding is harder to reconcile with the scientific approach to morality, as it invokes the notion of *telos* – typical for Aristotelian metaphysics – that is alien to contemporary science.

Second, the ontological sense of thesis about the negative character of evil is that whatever exists is good. This claim may be justified in two different ways. It is a direct consequence of the Christian claim that what was created by God is good. It may also be viewed as a consequence of the claim that whatever exists has measure, form, order – things that are unquestionably good – and thereby itself is good (things create a hierarchy of goodness: they may be more or less good, but nothing is bad in itself). Accordingly, once all goodness (and thereby measure, form and order) is removed, nothing 'positive' is retained – nature itself disappears. Both lines of argumentation can be discerned, for instance, in St Augustine's *De natura boni*. Clearly, these theological considerations go beyond the perspective assumed in this book, but they are, of course, not incompatible with it: there is no inconsistency in being at the same time an evolutionist and a theist.

6.2 The Kantian Account

Immanuel Kant did not use the term 'double ambivalence' in his account of human nature, especially regarding the sources of human evil, but his account is similar to the one proposed in this book in two main points: first, it is neither optimistic nor pessimistic, but ambivalent, and implies that human beings have certain propensities for evil but not for absolute evil, that is, they do not pursue evil for its own sake; second, it states that a moral transformation is necessary for human beings to become truly moral.

In his book *Die Religion innerhalb der Grenzen der bloßen Vernunft*, Kant distinguishes three types of human propensity towards evil. The least serious type is frailty (*fragilitas*), which is an agent's weakness in observing the rules he has accepted; it is a weakness of will consisting in the fact that even though an agent wants to comply with the rules *for the right reasons* (that is, simply because they are moral rules), he fails to realize his intention because of the greater motivational force of some other (amoral or immoral) motives. Frailty is therefore yielding to a temptation to follow one's amoral or immoral inclinations, and thereby to violate a moral rule. A more serious type is impurity (*impuritas*, *improbitas*): an agent is 'impure' if she observes moral rules not only 'out of duty', that is, just because they are moral rules, but also for some other reason; for instance, she may be telling the truth not only because it is a moral duty but also because she is afraid that her lying will be detected and punished. Impurity is therefore a tendency to contaminate the motives of our moral actions by including among them immoral or amoral motives. As a result of this contamination, our moral actions are only legal (in accordance with the duty), not moral in the strict sense (done only out of duty). The improper reason for action may in fact be stronger that the proper one – that of acting for the sake of duty. However, Kant does not analyse more closely the relation between 'proper' and 'improper' reasons in the motivation set of a morally 'impure' agent (that is, he does not analyse the problem of the gradation of impurity); for instance, he does not examine whether proper and improper reasons operate simultaneously, or whether the stronger reason 'switches off' the weaker one. It is noteworthy that, according to Kant, impurity is morally worse than frailty even though an impure person acts in accordance with a moral rule and a frail person fails to do so. This 'ranking' of propensities for evil can be explained by the fact that the frail person tries to perform the moral duty for the right reason (even if she fails in her efforts), while an impure person performs the moral duty for the (partly) wrong reason, and, for Kant, the crucial factor for the moral evaluation of an act is its motivation. In order for this ranking to be plausible, however, frailty cannot consist in yielding to *any* temptation to act amorally or immorally; it must be a temptation to do something which is only moderately wrong, such as to experience sensual pleasure. Kant does not make this point clear, but only in this way can his ranking be defended. The most reprehensible type of propensity for evil is wickedness or perversity (*vitositas*, *corruptio*), which consists in an agent prioritizing egoism (self-interest, self-love) over the moral law, and following the moral law only if it serves his own interest. It is therefore a tendency to invert the proper hierarchy of motives of action (there does not exist any reason, according to Kant, which would justify deviation from the moral law). Kant does not analyse at greater length the relations between impurity and wickedness, which may be interpreted in two different ways. On one interpretation, the difference between them consists in that, in the case of conflict between self-interest and moral law, the impure agent gives priority to the moral law, whereas the wicked agent gives priority to self-interest. In other words, in the case of such a conflict, the moral law plays no role in the motivational set of the wicked person, and plays a decisive role in that of the impure person. On this interpretation, one cannot be at the same time impure and wicked. But this interpretation implies that an 'impure' agent becomes 'pure' (that is, 'silences' his egoism) in the case of a conflict of motives, which is contradictory to the assumption that his motives are always contaminated. Besides, it would be rather strange that an agent who cannot act for the right reason when his motives point, so to say, in the same direction, can act for the right reason if they point at different courses of action. The second – more plausible – interpretation of the relations between impurity and wickedness assumes that impurity implies wickedness: the very fact that the agent is impure, that is, acts in accordance with the moral duty only if he has some additional motive (other than the willingness to obey the duty) to do so, implies that in the case of the conflict between moral duty and self-interest she will give priority to the latter. Impurity and wickedness would therefore be two sides of the same coin: the term 'impurity' stresses the fact that the agent can never follow moral duty for the right reasons (he always needs an additional – nonmoral – motive to act morally), and the term 'wickedness' stresses the fact that in the case of the conflict between moral and nonmoral motives, the agent will give priority to the latter. The latter fact seems to follow from the former because a motive which can never act independently (one such motive is willingness to follow a moral rule) cannot have priority over the motive which can act independently (one such motive is self-interest). By way of digression, it may be interesting to invoke Lars Svendsen's apt observation that Kant's account of propensity for evil, though extremely insightful, does not embrace two other – all too frequent – propensities for evil, viz. propensity for moralistic (idealistic) evil, in the case of which 'the agent believes that he represents the good and his victims are evil', and propensity for thoughtless (stupid) evil, in the case of which 'an agent does not stop to think about whether his actions are good or bad' (Svendsen 2011: 137).

In his analysis of human propensities for evil, Kant used the term 'radical evil'. The relation between this term and the three propensities for evil is not entirely clear. It seems that radical evil in a narrow sense is wickedness, and in a broader sense is also weakness and impurity. Irrespective of which of these two is assumed, radical evil in the Kantian sense proves to be a relatively moderate form of evil: 'radical' does not mean 'extreme' or 'absolute'. Kant does not maintain that the reason why human beings infringe upon moral duties is that they derive some demonic pleasure from the very fact of infringing upon moral duty; they are not therefore 'absolutely evil', that is, they do not commit evil just for the sake of committing evil. Kant straightforwardly denies that human beings may take the violation of moral rule to be the reason for their actions. The question arises why Kant, who denies 'absolute evil', employs the apparently misleading term 'radical evil' (resembling 'absolute evil') to describe human nature. Taken etymologically, however, the term is by no means misleading: as Kant reminds us, 'radix' means in Latin 'root', and the most typical human propensity for evil – impurity – consists precisely in contaminating the 'root' of our moral actions, viz. their motivation. Furthermore, the claim that the propensity towards evil is 'radical' means also that it is deeply rooted in human nature. It is not clear, however, whether it can be removed. Kant seems to have believed this possible, given that he believed in the *moral necessity* of a moral transformation of an agent. In Kant's philosophy, that something is morally required implies that it is morally possible; the principle 'Ought implies Can' is taken by him literally, as licensing the derivation of a factual statement (of what people can do) from a normative statement (of what they ought to do), or as licensing the transition from a normative statement (being a point of departure) to a factual statement. This is a nonstandard usage of this principle. In its standard usage, the principle is treated as a way of evaluating the plausibility of an 'Ought' statement by comparing it with a factual statement (being a point of departure) saying what people can do. In this usage, Kant's reasoning from 'Ought' to 'Can' is usually treated as unjustifiable – just like the reverse derivation, from the factual statement to the normative one. Kant would only agree that there is no transition from 'Is' (and its special case: 'Can') to 'Ought'.

Let me summarize. Kant's account of human evil is neither optimistic nor pessimistic. It is not optimistic because Kant admits that there exists in human nature a tendency to evildoing. But it is not pessimistic either, because Kant clearly states that human evil is not absolute evil: the human will is good, that is, it never wants to commit evil just because it is evil, and the worst evil which it can commit (prioritizing self-interest over the moral law) is far from being extreme. Human nature is therefore ambivalent, and as such needs to be 'transformed' if it is to become truly moral. Individual human beings must undergo a moral transformation/revolution, which will enable them to follow moral rules for proper reasons, that is, simply because they are moral rules. This moral revolution can be described, on the grounds of Kant's moral philosophy, in various ways: as coming to have a pure moral motivation (that is, performing the moral law just because it is the moral law); as gaining moral character, that is, a deep unity of personality, through a deep internalization of moral rules; or as developing a tendency to recognize the infinite value of each human agent, and thereby to treat him always as an end in itself and never merely as a means. In Kant's view, human beings are in a position to undergo such a transformation because they have free will. Kant also maintains that the very existence of various types of human propensity to evil is a result of a free decision by each individual human being (and that thereby we are responsible for having it), but he never explains how this is possible; he admits that this is a mystery which can only be made (partly) understandable if we invoke the theological doctrine of original sin. This is a somewhat puzzling fragment of Kant's considerations which I shall not analyse. I shall limit myself to noticing that the responsibility for our various types of propensity to evil would be plausible if it were understood not as responsibility for their arising but for their preservation: if we can remove our propensities (as Kant seems to believe), then we can be held responsible for them.

2. Progress in law: towards genuine ethics

1. FROM EVOLUTIONARY ETHICS TO GENUINE ETHICS

The process of overcoming our natural, imperfect ethics (evolutionary ethics), which generates what I have called secondary evil, and moving towards full-fledged genuine ethics was and is long and arduous. This process can be analysed both at the individual and the historical levels, because the moral transformation may be viewed both from the perspective of the development of an individual and from the perspective of the development of societies. Clearly, these two perspectives cannot be separated, because, for instance, it is easier to reach a higher level of moral development if one lives in a society accepting a moral system which is much 'above' evolutionary ethics. At the individual level the transition is construed as describing the stages of moral development of a given individual – an individual can be said to be morally mature if she or he has overcome the 'evolutionary stage' of morality and has internalized the principles of genuine ethics. As mentioned in the previous chapter, all the four basic components of evolutionary ethics need to be either forsaken or purified. Reciprocal altruism ethics can hardly be regarded as a mature form of ethics, as it is prudential (aimed at promoting the self-interest of the person practising it) and conditional. Tribal ethics is, even more obviously than reciprocal altruism ethics, an immature form of ethics, because its level of impartiality is disturbingly low: it relies on an arbitrary moral distinction between the members of one's group and the members of other groups (and therefore should be totally forsaken, not just purified). The same objection, though in a more moderate form, can be raised against family (kin altruism) ethics. Evolutionary ethics of empathy is also immature: the circle of persons included in it is too narrow. For all these reasons, evolutionary ethics cannot be regarded as genuine ethics, as a moral guide for a morally mature person; rather, it must be overcome. At the historical level, the differences between evolutionary ethics and genuine ethics can be fruitfully studied by examining the progress in legal systems. I shall assume this perspective in the following sections of this chapter. Here, meanwhile, I shall make two general remarks about progress in ethics: the first will concern the content of genuine ethics and the time when it developed; the second will concern the 'mental forces' which led to its development.

1.1 Axial Age Ethics as the Core of Genuine Ethics

The eminent German philosopher Karl Jaspers asserted that there were two main revolutions in the history of human thought: the ethical revolution in the Axial Age (800–300 BC), and the scientific revolution in the seventeenth century (Jaspers 2006: 34–6). The Axial Age was a time of spiritual revolution (the more or less simultaneous activity of such spiritual geniuses as Zoroaster, Confucius, Lao-Tse, Buddha, the Jewish prophets, and Socrates), which led to the emergence of a more developed form of ethics; the seventeenth century was a time of scientific genius which led to the emergence of mathematical natural sciences. Axial Age ethics developed in India, China, Israel, and Greece at a time of violence and as a reaction against this violence. As Karen Armstrong put it:

> The Axial sages developed their compassionate ethics in horrible and terrifying circumstances. They were not meditating in ivory towers but were living in frightening, war-torn societies, where the old values were disappearing … For instance, in Israel the Axial Age began after the destruction of Jerusalem and the enforced deportation of the exiles to Babylonia, where the priestly rulers started to explore an ideal of renunciation and ahimsa. In China the Axial Age developed during the Warring States period, when the Confucians, Mohists and Daoists all found ways to counteract widespread lawlessness and lethal aggression. In Greece it developed in the era of fighting poleis. (Armstrong 2006: 26)

Axial Age ethics can be interpreted as opposed not only to the immoral behaviours that directly preceded it (a traditional interpretation of this form of ethics) but also to the components of evolutionary ethics. A difference between these two interpretations can be more precisely presented as follows. At the historical level, Axial Age ethics arose in direct reaction to the amorality of the time of violence: it was directed against the 'ego principle' (prioritizing self-interest over the interests of other people) as a motive of human actions. At the conceptual level, Axial Age ethics can be opposed not only to the amorality of the time in which it arose but also to other types of ethics which are arguably embedded in human nature (and constitute evolutionary ethics), and thereby can be regarded as preceding it. I shall develop this interpretation by presenting at greater length – drawing especially on Armstrong (2006) – the distinct features of Axial Age ethics.

First, the Axial Age sages manifested a lack of concern for theoretical metaphysics: they stressed that what is important is not so much what you believe but what you do. Nonetheless, Axial Age ethics assumed what Armstrong called 'practical metaphysics'. Jaspers claimed that the Axial Age sages fully realized, and bravely faced, the existence of 'border situations' (*Grenzsituationen*), which led them to discover the tragic character of the human condition and of transcendence (cf. Jaspers 2006: 65). According to Jaspers, the Axial Age is characterized by 'austere greatness, creative lucidity, and the depth of sense' (Jaspers 2006: 34). Thus, the central tenet of this practical metaphysics was that life is essentially tragic, but this tragic character can be transcended to a certain extent if human beings abandon the 'ego principle' and start to pursue a self-effacing, compassionate lifestyle. This tenet was connected with the Axial Age sages' discovery of the inner self and 'inner transcendence' (as Armstrong calls it). This inner transcendence (called variously, in different religions, Nibbana, Dao, Atman, Brahman, or God) is believed to be achievable when one overcomes one's natural egoism, stepping outside one's ego.

Second, Axial Age ethics contained the requirement of universal concern for everybody, without limits. It therefore enabled transcending not only egoism, but also evolutionary ethics, with its limited concern for a narrow circle of people. The spirit of Axial Age ethics was therefore the spirit of (perfect) empathy: the evolutionary ethics of empathy is based on an underdeveloped (truncated or contaminated form of empathy), whereas Axial Age ethics is based on a full-fledged, perfect form of empathy.

Third, an essential component of Axial Age ethics was the Golden Rule. The Golden Rule has a positive and negative form: in the former it says 'do unto others as you would have them do unto you', therefore requiring that we look into ourselves to know what we desire and then do the same for others; in the latter it says 'do not unto others as you would not have them do unto you', therefore requiring that we look into ourselves to know what we do not desire and then do not do it to others. Since the Golden Rule was based on the assumption that no human being is better than others or deserves particularly special treatment or consideration, it was a means of overcoming the ego principle and thereby of achieving forgetting of the self and self-abasement (*kenosis*). As was argued by Karen Armstrong (2006: 208–9), the Golden Rule (in its negative version) was spelled out for the first time by Confucius (who called it *shu*). She recalls the following story. The disciples of Confucius asked him: 'What is the single thread that runs through all your teaching and pulls it all together?' He replied: 'Look into your own heart. Discover what it is that give you pain. And then refuse to inflict that pain on anybody else.' His disciples also asked: 'Master, which one of your teachings can we put into practice every day?' Confucius said: 'Do not do to others as you would not have them do to you.' Buddha preached the Golden Rule as well. It was also taught (in its positive version) by Jesus: 'So whatever you wish that others would do to you, do also to them, for this is the Law and the Prophets' (Matthew 7:12). And Rabbi Hillel the Elder maintained that the Golden Rule was the essence of Judaism.

It is worth comparing, at somewhat greater length, the Golden Rule with the rule of tit-for-tat (*TFT*; the essence of reciprocal altruism ethics). The Golden Rule (which is a protoversion of the Kantian categorical imperative) is categorical and unconditional. *TFT*, by contrast, can be viewed as a hypothetical, conditional version of the Golden Rule, as, on one of its formulations, it says: 'Do unto others as you would have them do unto you only if others do unto you as they would have you do unto them.' The contrast between the Golden Rule and *TFT* can also be described in the following way. *TFT* (as mentioned in Chapter 2) embraces the following rules: (1) start by cooperating; (2) do good to those who do good to you and do harm to those who do harm to you; (3) be (moderately) forgiving; (4) do not be (maliciously) envious. Now, the Golden Rule can be interpreted as assuming rules (1), (3) (perhaps without the qualification 'moderately') and (4), and a rule (2'): do good unconditionally. Let me repeat that the difference between the *TFT* rule and the Golden Rule is not superficial: while the former is a prudential, ego-centred rule, based on a conditional imperative of cooperation, the latter is a truly ethical rule, based on an unconditional imperative of cooperation. It should be noted here that the Golden Rule becomes fully plausible only if it is accompanied by empathy by which it can be corrected. The Golden Rule teaches us to treat our feelings and preferences as guides for treating other people; it therefore assumes that other human beings are uniform in terms of their reactions of pain and pleasure to various stimuli. But our feelings and preferences may be different from those of others. This is especially true regarding the positive version of the Golden Rule: while human beings avoid more or less similar things (for example, pain), they are often substantially different in their 'positive' desires. And it is precisely empathy that enables an agent to discern a situation when his preferences differ from the other person's preferences. Empathy is therefore a necessary supplement of the Golden Rule: without empathy the Golden Rule may lead to acting in a *bona fide* way which, however, brings results which are not beneficial for other persons. Of course, even if supplemented by empathy, the Golden Rule is not proof against abuses. For instance, Hans Kelsen (2003: 39) aptly remarked that I may wish the rule 'you can lie whenever you want' to be a general rule if I take myself to be so intelligent that I am sure that I can always detect lies told by other people. Accordingly, he claimed that the Golden Rule cannot be used as a subjective criterion of moral behaviour (that is, the criterion that takes into account how we wish that other people behave towards us) because it can be easily used as a justification of our immoral behaviour. It can only be used as an objective criterion: 'Behave towards other in such a way in which they *ought to* behave towards you.' But, as Kelsen remarked, this formulation of the Golden Rule assumes the existence of some criterion of moral behaviour, and therefore is empty. Thus, the Golden Rule either allows for the justification of immoral behaviour or is empty in content. But Kelsen's criticism of the Golden Rule, however penetrating, goes too far. What it shows is not that the Golden Rule is empty but rather that, in order to be a reliable guide of moral behaviour, it must go in tandem with a true willingness to act morally. But Kelsen is right that there are moral situations in which it can hardly be applied; for instance, 'no one wants to be punished, even when one has committed a crime. The Golden Rule therefore prohibits punishing the criminals' (Kelsen 2003: 39).

In summary, Jaspers' and Armstrong's claim that the Axial Age sages made a breakthrough in the history of ethics seems to be fully justified. But this breakthrough must be properly understood; some reservations must be set out.

First, it should not be conceived as meaning that it was not preceded by insights made by earlier thinkers. For instance, if one studies carefully the ethical thought of the sages of ancient Egypt or ancient Mesopotamia, one can discern in it some intimations of Axial Age ethics (cf. Jedynak 1972). It remains true, however, that there is a significant difference in the depth of ethical insights between the Axial Age sages and the earlier thinkers: the basic tenet of the Axial Age ethics – that the circle of people to whom we owe moral duties should be expanded – was not formulated with equal clarity and force (the metaphor of 'expanding moral circle', which I have used, was coined by the nineteenth-century historian William Lecky and popularized especially by Peter Singer (1981)).

Second, the range of the Axial Age revolution was limited to relatively few – so to say, the ethically most enlightened – people: Axial Age ethics did not become part of the common consciousness. Evidence of this is provided by the fact that the legal texts started to reflect genuine ethics in the relatively recent stages of the development of law (as we shall see more clearly in Section 4 of this chapter).

Third, and most importantly, the Axial Age ethics was not the 'final stage' in the progress of ethics (which is why I have dubbed it the 'core' of genuine ethics). Its basic rules – (perfect) empathy, universal benevolence, the Golden Rule – have remained the lasting achievements of ethical reflection but they were enriched thereafter by further developments, such as those brought about by Christianity: such ethical demands as those of humility, abstaining from all kinds of evil thought, or returning good for evil were emphasized more strongly by Christians than by the Axial Age sages (I write more about the originality of Christian ethical teaching later). Furthermore, given the historical context of the origins of Axial Age ethics, it did not contain many of the more specific rules which belong to genuine ethics (such as those proclaiming concern for future generations), and some of the rules accepted by the Axial Age sages are not aspects of genuine ethics but relics of evolutionary ethics (such as those legitimizing the lower social status of women). I shall present those more specific elements of genuine ethics not contained in Axial Age ethics while discussing the progress made in law.

Fourth, as we have seen, religion played an important, even crucial, role in the process of discovering the rules of genuine ethics (the Axial Age sages were also religious reformers). It must be admitted, however, that the role of religion in ethical progress was not always positive. One may plausibly argue that, for instance, a badly understood Christian doctrine or religious fanaticism may have justified, to some extent, the cruel punishments often handed down, with their focus on mutilation and degradation (of which I shall have more to say in Section 4). The propagators of these punishments (such as the stake, pillory, quartering) argued that such treatment may be good for the soul of the convict, since the suffering they inflicted on him would 'purify' his soul and thus protect him from eternal suffering; that is, the more he suffered in this world, the less he would have to suffer in the afterlife (cf. Sójka-Zielińska 2000: 77). As the Polish historian Janusz Tazbir put it: 'imprisonment and death did not mean a lot if they were considered as being endowed with transcendent sense – as constituting a penance for sins and therefore a condition of redemption' (Tazbir 1993: 44). The broad topic of religion's influence on the development of ethics deserves, of course, more in-depth treatment; however, that would go beyond the scope of this book.

1.2 The Role of Reason and Emotion in Discovering Genuine Ethics

It is fascinating to question whether progress in ethics was propelled more by reason or by emotions (the role of religious insight was mentioned in the previous section). Arguably, it was reason that played a more important role in this process. Its basic moral task (if not already performed by religion) is to make us aware that, as Adam Smith put it, 'we are but one of the multitude, in no respect better than any other in it, and that when we prefer ourselves so shamefully and blindly to others, we become the proper objects of resentment, abhorrence and execration' (Smith 2007: 171). This moral discovery, amounting to the radical overcoming of the 'ego principle', is the cornerstone of genuine ethics. A similar view on the role of reason in making moral discoveries has been endorsed by many thinkers. For instance, Steven Pinker, while analysing the role of philosophers in the 'humanitarian revolution' (of which I shall write in Section 4 of this chapter), wrote:

> With enough scrutiny by disinterested, rational and informed thinkers, these practices [cruel punishment, slavery, and so on – WZ] cannot be justified indefinitely. The universe of ideas, in which one idea entails others, is itself an exogenous force, and once a community of thinkers enters that universe, they will be forced in certain directions regardless of their material surroundings. It is a process of moral discovery. (Pinker 2011: 180)

He also used the felicitous term 'escalation of reason', underlining the processual character of these discoveries (for example, abolishing mistaken views about women, such as that they are less intelligent; about different races, such as that some of them are better than others; about animals, such as that they do not experience pain; about homosexual people, such as that they choose their sexual orientation). The eminent legal philosopher Herbert L.A. Hart wrote in similar vein:

> No doubt the contention that a legal system must treat all human beings within its scope as entitled to certain basic protections and freedoms, is now generally accepted as a statement of an ideal of obvious relevance in the criticism of law. Even where practice departs from it, lip service to this ideal is usually forthcoming. It may even be the case that a morality which does not take this view of the right of all men to equal consideration can be shown by philosophy to be involved in some inner contradiction, dogmatism, or irrationality. If so, the enlightened morality which recognizes these rights has special credentials as the true morality, and is not just one among many possible moralities. (Hart 1994: 206)

The role of reason in ethical development was also emphasized by Charles Darwin:

> As man gradually advanced in intellectual power, and was enabled to trace the more remote consequences of his actions; as he acquired sufficient knowledge to reject baneful customs and superstitions; as he regarded more and more, not only the welfare, but the happiness of his fellow-men; as from habit, following on beneficial experience, instruction and example, his sympathies became more tender and widely diffused, extending to men of all races, to the imbeciles, maimed, and other useless members of society, and finally to the lower animals, so would the standard of his morality rise higher and higher. (Darwin 1871: 84)

Some other conclusions flow from the claim about the crucial role played by reason in discovering moral rules. I have argued that in the course of history our empathy has developed (towards what I have called 'perfect empathy'). This observation is true but only if properly understood. The progress does not appear to have consisted in the increase of our emotional sensitivity but rather in internalizing, by dint of the activity of reason, moral rules which enable us to counteract some defects of (natural) empathy, especially its partiality (though not another defect, which is its relative *affective* weakness). If the development of empathy is above all the result of the development of moral rules, it means that we may have a larger influence on the quality of our empathy than is usually assumed. We may not be able to decide to increase the affective strength of our empathic reactions towards those who we regard as proper objects of empathy, but we are able to accept and internalize moral norms which broaden the circle of people who are the objects of our moral concern, subsequently leading to the development of empathy itself (by reducing its partiality). This claim is in fact very intuitive: empathy towards a given person, similarly to any other emotion, depends on what we think about this person; and what we think is to a large extent a function of the moral rules we accept. As was aptly noticed by Steven Pinker: 'sympathy is endogenous, an effect rather than a cause of how people relate to one another. Depending on how beholders conceive of a relationship, their response to another person's pain may be empathic, neutral, or even counter empathic' (Pinker 2011: 578). And in similar vein:

> In the modern West, the avoidance of some kinds of violence, such as mercy-killing an abandoned child, retaliating for an insult, declaring war on another developed state, consists not in weighing the moral issues, empathizing with the targets, or restraining an impulse, but in not having the violent act as a live option in the mind at all. The act is not considered and avoided; it is unthinkable and laughable. (Pinker 2011: 624)

Accordingly, progress in morality does not consist, in the first place, in progress in the *affective strength* of empathy (which may have not altered considerably) but rather in progress in the content of moral rules (and, consequently, in progress in the range of empathy). This progress also consists in 'blocking', by appropriate moral rules, the primitive reactions of anger (leading to the desire for vengeance), disgust and contempt which suspend our empathy. For instance, owing to the process of 'moralization' (described in Section 3.1 of Chapter 1), some categories of human beings which elicited disgust or contempt, such as people with dwarfism, mentally ill people, crippled people or those performing 'unclean' professions, were for a long time not included in the category of human beings deserving respect and consideration; in fact, they were often not even considered as fully human beings.

The above considerations should not be interpreted as downplaying the role of emotions (including empathy) in our moral decisionmaking. They imply that the moral development of emotions is secondary to progress in moral reflection, not that a genuinely ethical person will be guided only, or above all, by reason (that is, a sense of duty, respect for moral rules). Thus, though I agree with Pinker's analysis of relations between reason and empathy, I cannot share his (normative) claim that 'the ultimate goal should be policies and norms that become second nature and render empathy unnecessary' (Pinker 2011: 592). Even though such sceptical distance towards the 'emotional side' of human nature seems to be, in general, justified (as I argued in Section 3.1 of Chapter 1), it nonetheless goes too far. Insightful remarks on the interplay between reason and emotions in motivating our behaviour were made by Adam Smith. He claimed that as regards benevolent emotions (passions), moral rules should have only a subsidiary, corrective role, and the dominant motive should be the emotions themselves. By contrast, with unsocial emotions, moral rules should be motivating: we should, for instance, punish other people reluctantly, mainly to comply with rules, and the unsocial emotion which motivates punishment (anger, for example) ought to be pushed to the background. Smith was, however, realistic about the possibility of cultivating benevolent emotions on the part of a large number of people. As he claimed, few people have very sensitive emotions, but, fortunately, almost everyone can learn to act according to rules (even though, as Smith stressed, altruistic action motivated by rules is less perfect than altruistic action motivated by proper sentiments, because only in the latter case can the agent notice all morally relevant details of a given situation and make his action fully adequate to this situation's 'moral requirements').

In the remaining sections of this chapter I shall deal with the progress in law towards the pattern of rules provided by genuine ethics. I shall start by presenting two general implications for understanding the law of the view of human nature that is defended in the book.

2. THE DOUBLE AMBIVALENCE OF HUMAN NATURE AND THE PROGRESS IN LAW

The first implication of the picture of human nature proposed in Chapter 2 is that the law is both necessary and possible. If the picture were *very* optimistic, the law would not be necessary: people would not act egoistically and there would be no serious conflicts of interest between them. If it were *very* pessimistic, the law would not be possible: as David Hume noticed, in the state in which there dominated extreme malevolence – 'desperate rapaciousness: such a disregard to equity, such contempt of order, such stupid blindness to future consequences' (Hume 1998: 86), justice (which is tantamount to law in his account) could not be realized. The pessimistic picture could also be invoked (as many extremely conservative thinkers did in the past, for example Joseph de Maistre) to justify an antidemocratic, authoritarian regime, which would ruthlessly curb people's immoral and destructive instincts. The second implication, which is much more interesting than the first one, is connected with the question whether the law is expressive of human nature or counteracts it. In order to clearly answer this question, one must distinguish between two types of legal rules. The first layer embraces the elementary rules, that is, those rules which are indispensable for the survival of society. The second layer embraces the rules which regulate those matters which are not directly connected with the survival of society (for example, the status of women or of illegitimate children, the form of marriage, the political regime). In general, primitive legal systems are to a large extent expressive of human nature: rules belonging to both layers are correlates of natural propensities. The same cannot be said about more developed legal systems, which either (ethically) purify the rules expressive of human nature or replace them with rules which are directly contrary to human nature. Let me develop the distinction between the two layers of legal rules at greater length.

The rules of the first layer correspond to what Herbert L.A. Hart dubbed 'the minimum content of natural law'. They are necessary for the realization of the 'minimum purpose of survival which men have in associating with each other' (Hart 1994: 193). The assumption of the purpose constitutes an element of teleology in Hart's theory (as he himself admits), but this teleology is very modest, as it is limited only to the purpose of survival, and the identification of this purpose is not based on any metaphysical speculations but 'rests on the simple contingent fact that most men most of the time wish to continue in existence' (Hart 1994: 191). Hart reconstructs this content by first enumerating certain features of human nature/condition which may work against survival (he calls the statements describing these features 'truisms'), and then by reflecting on the legal rules necessary to counteract the destructive potential of these features. The features (in conjunction with the assumed purpose of survival) constitute reasons why 'law and morals should include a specific content' (Hart 1994: 193). Hart writes:

> in the absence of this content men, as they are, would have no reason for obeying voluntarily any rules; and without a minimum of co-operation given voluntarily by those who find that it is in their interest to submit to and maintain the rules, coercion of others who would not voluntarily conform would be impossible. (Hart 1994: 193)

The first feature – human vulnerability to bodily attack – is counteracted by rules that proscribe or restrict the use of physical violence, for example, by the rule 'thou shalt not kill'. The second feature is approximate equality in 'physical strength, agility, and intellectual capacities'; it means that no individual is 'so much more powerful than others, that he is able, without co-operation, to dominate or subdue them for more than a short period of time' and begets a need for a 'system of mutual forbearance and compromise which is the base of both legal and moral obligation' (Hart 1994: 195). The third feature – limited altruism – makes rules of mutual forbearance necessary and possible: if people were devils, they would be impossible, and if they were angels, they would be unnecessary. The fourth feature – that of limited resources – is counteracted by 'some minimal form of the institution of property (though not necessarily individual property), and the distinctive kind of rule which requires respect for it' (Hart 1994: 196), as well as rules concerning contracts (for example, prescribing promise-keeping). Finally, human beings exhibit weakness of will and limited understanding of their long-term interests, which tempt them into antisocial actions; thus, in order to guarantee their compliance with legal rules, sanctions for their violation are necessary. In summary: rules that constitute the minimum content of natural law serve the 'protection of persons, property and promises' (Hart 1994: 196).

Several observations need to be made on Hart's minimum content of natural law.

First, Hart does not make a distinction between truisms which provide reasons for accepting a specific content of legal rules and those which make the whole legal system possible and necessary. The truisms of the first type are human vulnerability and limited resources (which justify rules respecting person, property and promises), while those of the second type are approximate equality, limited altruism and limited understanding and weakness of will (they are therefore connected with the first implication presented at the beginning of this section). Hart also does not make a distinction between a legal system which does not protect the purpose of survival and one which directly attacks this purpose. But this distinction does not seem to be important: it just shows that one may have weaker or stronger reasons for disobeying the law.

Second, the term 'natural law' as used by Hart in his considerations about 'minimum content of natural law' has a different meaning than that commonly used by natural law theorists. The rules that constitute 'the minimum content' are in fact hypothetical rules of the following form: 'if you want to achieve the goal of survival, you ought to follow rules *a*, *b*, *c* …' They are therefore 'demystified': their source has nothing mysterious or sublime in it; they are simply means for achieving survival, and they can be found empirically – by testing various rules as to their aptitude for serving the survival of society. It is worth noticing that there is a certain similarity between Thomas Hobbes's theory of natural law and Hart's theory; as Leo Strauss aptly noted, 'Hobbes made an unconditional natural right [to self-survival – WZ] the basis of all natural duties, the duties being therefore only conditional' (Strauss 1965: 182). In Hart's theory, the duties are also conditional, though the goal of survival is not treated as an unconditional natural right. One can therefore say that Hart's theory is even more distant from classical natural law theory than Hobbes's.

Third, the law respecting the minimum content of natural law can be deeply unjust. As Hart puts it:

> It is plain that neither the law nor the accepted morality of societies need extend their minimal protections and benefits to all within their scope, and often they have not done so. In slave-owning societies the sense that the slaves were human beings, not mere objects to be used, may be lost by the dominant group, who may yet remain morally most sensitive to each other's claims and interests. (…) Even where slavery is not officially recognized, discrimination on grounds of race, colour, or creed may produce a legal system and a social morality which does not recognize that all men are entitled to a minimum protection from others. These painful facts of human history are enough to show that, though society to be viable must offer *some*

> of its members a system of mutual forbearances, it need not, unfortunately, offer them to all. (Hart 1994: 200–1)

To return to more general considerations: it seems that the development of law can be viewed as a steady replacement of the rules expressive of human nature by the rules expressive of various moral discoveries. This general hypothesis is confirmed by a close analysis of the development of legal systems: the analysis shows that the rules (both of the first and second layer) which are part of evolutionary ethics have a tendency to become purified or to disappear from legal systems. I shall divide my presentation of this development into two parts. In Section 3 I shall discuss an evolution of legal systems towards moral egalitarianism, that is, towards the discovery that each human being has an equal value. This discovery is a fundamental assumption of contemporary (Western) legal systems: it provides a justification of democracy and underlies these systems' more specific rules, which I discuss in Section 4.

3. PROGRESS TOWARDS MORAL EGALITARIANISM

At the dawn of human history, and through much of its early part (until the Neolithic revolution), human beings lived in egalitarian societies – in bands or tribes. Egalitarian structure can therefore be regarded as a natural or at least a primitive form of the organization of human societies. But from some time after the Neolithic revolution (that is, after the invention of agriculture) until the twentieth century, the dominant organizational form of society became nonegalitarian (cf. Betzig 2008). The evolution of human society structures can therefore be described, from a bird's-eye view, as having proceeded from egalitarianism to nonegalitarianism and back to egalitarianism. Since the egalitarian structure was historically the earliest one, it can be regarded as natural, although, interestingly, it is 'unnatural' when seen in a broader context of the dominant structures of primate communities – which, with few exceptions, are strongly hierarchical. The question then arises about the psychological bases of human egalitarianism. I shall argue that the bases of primitive and contemporary egalitarianism are essentially different. The former can be traced back to our propensities shaped by natural selection, whereas the latter are 'unnatural' – they are connected with moral discoveries and the appearance of genuine ethics.

3.1 The Nonethical Bases of Primitive Egalitarianism

Broadly speaking, one can distinguish two types of hypotheses aimed at explaining the psychological bases of primitive egalitarianism: hypotheses of one type assume that the human mind is a blank slate with respect to political behaviour, whereas hypotheses of the other type assume that the human mind is more like a slate covered with numerous inscriptions left by evolutionary forces. I shall analyse the hypotheses of the second type at greater length. I discount the hypotheses of the first type for the following three reasons. First, in light of evolutionary theory it is not convincing to maintain that the human mind is a blank slate with respect to any kind of behaviour, including political behaviour. Second, the purely economic or social hypotheses (that is, hypotheses appealing to factors external to human nature, for example to demographic instability, rather than to human nature itself) can be neither sufficient nor 'ultimate'. As was noticed by Christopher Boehm:

> There is little doubt that demographic instability, nomadic restraints on material accumulation, absence of economic specialization outside the family, or uncentralized redistribution systems for meat [the most popular hypotheses of social and economic causes of primitive egalitarianism – WZ] are important, for they are widespread and universal. They unquestionably contribute to an egalitarian way of life, for they provide conditions friendly for the maintenance of egalitarian politics. But as leveling mechanisms, even in combination, they do not explain the totally predictable egalitarian ways of these mobile nomads – especially if we entertain the possibility that humans are 'naturally' hierarchical. (Boehm 2001: 38)

Furthermore:

> These forager-specific hypotheses do not help at all in explaining the fact that many other nonliterate people, who live in permanent, settled groups that accumulate food surpluses through agriculture, are quite similar politically … these tribesmen lack strong leadership and domination among adult males, they make their decisions by consensus, and they too exhibit an egalitarian ideology. This is the case even though (1) they are not nomadic; (2) they do not necessarily share meat or other food beyond the family; (3) they are in a favorable position to accumulate material goods; (4) their group composition can be highly stable; (5) some exhibit a degree of economic specialization. The fact that tribesmen are ecologically and socially quite different from foragers, but remain similarly egalitarian, requires a more general explanation. The question is one of ultimate causality: a single cause or a set of causes is needed to explain a widespread political phenomenon. (Boehm 2001: 38)

Third, hypotheses of the first type are also contrary to our knowledge about our closest primate relatives – nonhuman primates, which, as has been mentioned, prove to have a highly developed 'political nature'.

I shall now present three main hypotheses of the second type, which try to provide 'an ultimate cause', that is, to embed primitive egalitarianism in some tendencies of human nature. At the outset, however, I should explain why I shall not take into account the hypothesis which asserts that the 'psychological force' underlying primitive egalitarianism is human desire for freedom. The desire for freedom may mean desire for either political or nonpolitical freedom (cf. Eliasz, Załuski 2017). The desire for political freedom is in fact equivalent *either* to the propensity for egalitarianism – and therefore cannot be invoked as a separate hypothesis, since Hypothesis 1 postulates the existence of such a propensity in human nature – *or* to 'aversion to being dominated', 'the disinclination to obey', in which case, again, it cannot be invoked as a separate hypothesis, since the existence of 'aversion to being dominated' is part of Hypothesis 3. So, perhaps, the desire for nonpolitical freedom may give rise to a different hypothesis explaining the emergence of egalitarianism? It cannot be denied that people desire nonpolitical – negative – freedom, that is, they desire a lack of obstacles in realizing their basic goals, but this sphere of negative freedom is in fact respected in egalitarian and nonegalitarian societies. Accordingly, it seems that even in despotic states this basic sphere of negative freedom was respected. The only true exception to this came in totalitarian states, but there were few of these across human history and their 'lifespans' were short – precisely because they did not respect this basic sphere of human freedom. Thus, the desire for nonpolitical freedom is useless as a basis of explanation of primitive societies' egalitarian character.

Let me now move on to more detailed discussion of the dominant hypotheses of the second type.

Hypothesis 1: Human beings are by nature egalitarian, free from hierarchical propensities. The primitive egalitarianism is therefore a direct expression of human nature. The collapse of egalitarianism and the transition to hierarchical societies can only be explained by external factors, for example, the invention of private property, agriculture, or metallurgy.

This view was defended, for example, by Jean-Jacques Rousseau (1969) and Friedrich Engels (2006). The weak point of this hypothesis is that it denies the existence of hierarchical propensities in human nature, which seem to be its essential aspect. That the human drive for dominance is very real is shown by the fact that this drive gained the upper hand over most of human history after the Neolithic revolution: only a small percentage of states possessed a democratic, egalitarian structure, most of them being instead despotic or authoritarian (the contemporary world is exceptional in this regard). Furthermore, as has been proven by ethnographic and anthropologic research, egalitarian communities were by no means free from inner tensions and conflicts; in order to sustain an egalitarian structure, community members had to exhibit constant vigilance so as to detect and counteract tendencies of potential 'alphas' to dominate them. Also highly contentious was Engels's claim (based on Lewis Henry Morgan's research summarized in his *Ancient Society*) that primitive egalitarian societies were 'protocommunistic', that is, property was held communally in them, and 'promiscuous', that is, the institution of marriage (in any of its many possible forms) did not exist and sexual relationships were unregulated. But, of course, this 'double claim' of Engels is logically independent from Hypothesis 1's essential claim that human beings are by nature egalitarian. It should be noted, however, that there seems to be some grain of truth in Engels's claim that property was held communally in primitive societies: indeed, property usually belonged to a special kind of communal – kin – group, and could not be sold or divided between individuals. Furthermore, Rousseau's version of Hypothesis 1 is erroneous because it assumes that human beings are by nature 'individualistic', which is incompatible with the view of human beings supported by biological sciences; according to this view, human beings are by nature 'social', predestined to live in groups.

Hypothesis 2: Envy can be invoked to explain the origins and the maintenance of primitive egalitarianism as well as the maintenance of hierarchical societies.

The account of man as *homo invidiosus* was developed in the historical–sociological context by the German sociologist Helmut Schoeck (1987). According to Schoeck, envy is a powerful psychological force and led both to the rise and the preservation of egalitarianism. The causal process proceeded, according to Schoeck, in two interconnected ways. First, humans' fear of others' envy led to conformism – to a reluctance to 'stand out'. The imperative governing egalitarian societies was: 'Behave so that the result of your actions will arouse the minimum envy in your fellow men' (Schoeck 1987: 68). Second, envy of others' social and economic positions enabled an effective social control. Schoeck (1987: 58–9) advanced an additional claim that the fear of envy was one of the greatest barriers to innovation in primitive societies and thereby the main reason for their static character. He also invoked the view of man as *homo invidiosus* in explaining the stability of strongly hierarchical societies. He argued that the hypothesis of *homo invidiosus* is not falsified by the fact that throughout a large part of history human beings lived in despotic societies because envy is 'sensitive' to social proximity: it is usually directed only towards persons with whom it has been possible to compete. Consequently, 'overwhelming and astounding inequality, especially when it has an element of the unattainable, arouses far less envy than minimal inequality, which inevitably causes the envious man to think: "I might also be in his place"' (Schoeck 1987: 77). And in similar vein: 'Societies up to now have developed various methods of keeping envy within bounds: positive law, religions that preach renunciation or the hope of compensation in another world, theory of an innately superior elite, conceptions of capricious fate' (Schoeck 1987: 302). Moreover, the second-best option for the envious person is the one in which there is only one person (despot) or at least few persons who will be envied; envy is, so to say, 'satisfied' by equality with the bulk of the members of society.

Schoeck's observations are interesting and insightful but, apparently, he overstated the explanatory potential of envy (all the more given that, as I argued in Section 2.2 of Chapter 1, malicious envy can hardly be regarded as part of our 'biological nature'): by focusing exclusively on envy, he neglected the hierarchical propensities in human nature. But it cannot be denied that envy (just or benign) could have played an important role in generating primitive egalitarianism and in preserving it, and it is to Schoeck's great merit that he drew our attention to this fact.

There is also a strand of psychological reductionism in Schoeck's analysis. He tried to argue that 'the sense of equity, of justice and injustice is inherent in man because of his capacity for envy' (Schoeck 1987: 298). On this account, a sense of justice arises in the agent as a result of her envy caused by receiving less than others and her anticipation of others' envy when she receives more than others, and thereby from her willingness to avoid conflicts with them. This reductionist account of justice, however, is not very convincing. It is based on an implausible assumption that those who make claims for justice are motivated by envy. It is patently implausible in the case of nonegalitarian justice. As Max Scheler (1997: 171–3), rightly noted, justice understood 'proportionally' – as a requirement of treating equal people equally and unequally people unequally – cannot be a result of envy. But it is also implausible as a general truth about motivation for egalitarian justice. Many egalitarian thinkers or activists had no reason to feel envy, as they were well off, and it was in their material interest that the inequalities were preserved. Furthermore, it does not take into account the fact that claims for egalitarian justice may be a result of moral indignation rather than envy.

Hypothesis 3: *Human beings have been endowed by natural selection with hierarchical propensities (the will to dominate and the aversion to being dominated) but these propensities in conjunction with instrumental rationality and the capacity for symbolic thinking lead to egalitarianism.*

This hypothesis was put forward by Christopher Boehm (2001, 2012). In striving to explain the egalitarian character of primitive societies, Boehm appeals to insights regarding human nature provided by evolutionary theory, especially to the insight that human beings display a drive for dominance and an aversion to domination. Now, this insight underlies the following reasoning (developed by Boehm in his book *Hierarchy in the Forest*) which could have led human beings to opt for egalitarianism: each person desires to be at the top of the social hierarchy, but because he has little chance of realizing this desire (others have similar desires), he prefers to live in an egalitarian society (in which he cannot dominate but has at least the guarantee that he will not be dominated) than in a hierarchical society (in which he *can* dominate, but there is little chance of it: the more probable scenario is that he will be dominated). Thus, his preference ordering is as follows: to dominate > to be equal > to submit to alpha > to fight with alpha and lose; the rational choice here is 'to be equal'. The preference for egalitarianism is therefore a result of a simple logic of instrumental rationality – the logic concisely summarized by Henry Schneider (cited by Boehm): 'All men seek to rule, but if they cannot rule they prefer to remain equal.' To achieve such a structure, agents ('the rank and file') must combine their forces by forming a coalition, which enables them to effectively oppose – to 'dominate' – potential alphas; as Boehm writes, 'egalitarian society is the product of a large, well-united coalition of subordinates who boldly deny political power to the would-be alphas in their group' (Boehm 2001: 157). According to Boehm, therefore, human aversion to domination is a powerful equalizing force: it underlies an egalitarian character of primitive human societies. It is worth noting that, on Boehm's view, it is not the case that egalitarian primitive societies lacked any kind of social hierarchy. The hierarchy in those societies was, in his view, simply reversed: at the top of this hierarchy there were the 'rank and file', whose power lay in their capacity to act together against the would-be alphas, and at the bottom there were those would-be alphas. Boehm calls this hierarchy 'the reverse social dominance hierarchy'. Traditional hierarchy can be depicted in the form of a normal pyramid, and egalitarian hierarchy in the form of a reverse pyramid.

As mentioned, egalitarianism of primitive human societies is something exceptional in the world of primates. Boehm explains the fact that human beings managed to create and maintain egalitarian order by pointing out that only human beings – thanks to their unique cognitive capacity for symbolic thinking – could create a moral community based on an egalitarian ethos, which – in his view – was necessary to support egalitarianism as a viable political structure. This ethos provided justification for, for example, various means of punishing authoritarian individuals ('potential alphas'), such as public criticism, ridicule, ostracism and even physical elimination. Thus, apart from hierarchical propensities, the capacity for symbolic thinking (made possible by the development of a large brain) is the main causal factor which, in Boehm's view, stands behind the emergence of the egalitarian structures. But he also mentions other factors which facilitated this process, viz. the invention of hunting weapons, which 'made men more dangerous to one another and thereby mitigated the differences of size and strength in fighting' (Boehm 2011: 173), and the advent of large-game hunting, which intensified human cooperation. This last factor is particularly emphasized by Boehm in his book *Moral Origins*.

Boehm formulated two other hypotheses in addition to his core hypothesis about the origins of egalitarianism: that primitive egalitarianism was a selective pressure shaping human altruistic traits; and that primitive egalitarianism empowered selection at the between-group level. In *Hierarchy in the Forest* Boehm explicitly combines these two claims, writing that primitive egalitarianism favoured the development of altruistic traits because it empowered selection at the between-group level (by decreasing within-group selection through elimination of alpha males and by sharpening the differences between groups), while in *Moral Origins* he separates these claims, focusing on the way (which he calls 'social selection') in which, in his view, primitive egalitarianism may have affected the selection of altruistic traits 'taking place between individuals *within* groups' (Boehm 2012: 13). Thus, in *Moral Origins* Boehm suggests that the selection of altruistic traits took place at individual rather than group level. He argues that social selection can be divided into two submechanisms, viz., selection by reputation and punitive selection (social control). The former mechanism directly favours altruistic genes (agents who manifest extrafamilial generosity obtain thereby a good reputation, which translates into enhanced chances of spreading their genes), whereas the latter mechanism favours them indirectly (because it leads to suppressing the fitness prospects of antisocial individuals: bullies and free-riders). Boehm's hypothesis of the role of social selection in shaping the gene pool supplements standard hypotheses such as reciprocal altruism, kin selection, sexual selection, or group selection. Interestingly, Boehm's hypothesis implies that evolutionary processes, at least in one case, are not quite 'blind', because 'unwittingly, hunter-gatherers' social intentions affect the gene pool in the direction of greater altruism' (Boehm 2012: 16). On the basis of this hypothesis, Boehm speculates about the origins of the human conscience. In opposition to Darwin's claim that conscience is a side effect of human intelligence and social instincts, he asserts that the human conscience evolved for a specific reason, viz., as a means of self-control enabling agents to avoid group punishment for bullying or cheating behaviour. Thus, according to Boehm, those individuals who were better at inhibiting their antisocial tendencies (who developed 'conscience') had a fitness advantage over those who manifested them openly. Boehm claims that his account of the origins of conscience implies that the 'optimal evolutionary conscience' is not morally perfect, that is, it does not lead to automatic following of moral rules but to opportunistic following, and thereby to breaking such rules whenever this does not involve a high risk of detection and punishment. This account is undoubtedly original, though it is not clear why, given his peculiar understanding of conscience (on the grounds of which one can call an immoral – rule-evading – behaviour dictated by conscience), Boehm believes that what is provided is an account of the origins of conscience rather than simply an account of the origins of self-control.

It is worth noting that the above discussed hypotheses imply slightly different views of primitive egalitarianism: Hypothesis 1 implies what is called 'relaxed' egalitarianism (because it denies the presence of hierarchical proclivities in human nature), whereas the remaining hypotheses imply what is called 'tense' egalitarianism – the form of an egalitarian structure which requires constant vigilance regarding, and often harsh sanctions (criticism, ridicule, social distancing, elimination) against, potential alphas – upstarts, bullies, aggressors. As Helmut Schoeck claimed, the 'communal spirit of unspoilt, simple societies is a myth' (Schoeck 1987: 64–5). Anthropological data confirm the more pessimistic hypothesis – that primitive egalitarianism has a 'tense' character. Furthermore, Hypothesis 1 implies that egalitarianism is a direct expression of our egalitarian propensities and thereby does not require egalitarian communities to be regarded as a product of human intentionality, that is, as cultural inventions or 'imagined communities', whereas the remaining hypotheses imply that egalitarianism cannot be just an expression of our egalitarian propensities because human nature also comprises nonmoral (hierarchical and envious) tendencies – it must therefore be a product of human intentionality. In general, intentionality need not be invoked to explain the political structure of those species whose 'political nature' is monolithic – either predominantly hierarchical or predominantly egalitarian. As Boehm writes:

> Intentionality and morality are not needed to form a despotic hierarchy, one in which strong dispositions to competitively dominate inevitably push certain individuals to the top. The despotic order of chickens, for example, is basically mechanical, with the pyramid of power pointing upward toward a few dominant individuals. Nor are complicated intentions or a use of ethics needed to form an egalitarian society like that of squirrel monkeys, in which innate dispositions to compete through dominance are so weak that much of the time little sign of hierarchy is apparent. This relaxed social order is equally mechanical. (Boehm 2001: 171)

Let me now move on to an evaluation of Boehm's key hypothesis about the origins of primitive egalitarianism. There is no doubt that it is original, insightful and, overall, convincing. It may, however, require some corrections or, rather, supplements. First, as was already mentioned in Section 3.2 of Chapter 2, Boehm's list of hierarchical propensities does not seem to be complete. Arguably, in addition to the desire to dominate and an aversion to being dominated, they also embrace the tendency to obey authority. Now, it seems that if neither of the two tendencies mentioned by Boehm, that is, the desire to dominate and an aversion to being dominated, can be realized – that is, if it is impossible to be a dominant individual and to establish an egalitarian social structure, or a structure in which there is a reverse social dominance hierarchy – the tendency to obey authority becomes 'actualized'. It seems that this evolved deferential disposition constitutes an important motive that directs agents to comply with legal norms which they do not accept and which they are disposed to violate, but with which the authority endowed with the power to enforce these norms demands compliance. Second, the psychological forces revealed by Boehm may have acted side by side with those emphasized by Schoeck. It seems, therefore, that Hypotheses 2 and 3 should be combined to build a more comprehensive account of the origins of primitive egalitarianism. But – and this is my third, and most important, point – their explanatory scope should be narrowly defined: they are adequate with respect to primitive egalitarianism, but not, as I shall argue in the next section, with respect to contemporary egalitarianism. The difference between primitive and contemporary egalitarianism is simply a manifestation of a more general difference: between evolutionary ethics and genuine ethics.

3.2 The Ethical Bases of Contemporary Egalitarianism

The ideology that underlies contemporary egalitarianism is essentially different from the egalitarian ethos which, according to Boehm, was typical of primitive egalitarianism. Boehm describes this ethos in purely prudential terms, so that it is dubious whether the community can indeed be called 'ethical'. As he wrote:

> This egalitarian ethos amounts to an unusual political 'game' that is based on social agreement among the main political actors. The implicit contract reads something like this. There are individually variable human tendencies to outstrip or control one's fellows, which can lead to domination by the strong. We determine to solve this problem as follows. Rather than countenance modes of competition that will permit one of us to dominate the others, we all agree to give up our statistically small chance of becoming ascendant – in order to avoid the very high probability that we will be subordinated. We agree to settle merely for individual autonomy for all, rather than seeking ascendancy or domination, and we implement this program by defining our 'firsts' as mere 'equals'. (Boehm 2001: 123–4)

The modern egalitarian ethos is entirely different – it is moral in character. It is based on several fundamental discoveries, forming an important part of genuine ethics, viz.: (1) that each individual, irrespective of her race, sex, nationality, education, and so on, has an equal moral value; (2) that this value is, if not infinite, then at least very great – of a qualitatively different nature than the value of other living organisms, so that every human being can be said to possess, by virtue of the very fact of his or her being human, moral dignity; (3) that, as a result, an individual is to be ranked higher than society, the state or other abstract entities. This basic moral discovery that all human beings have moral dignity, and that this dignity is equal in all of them, leads to the rejection of various forms of discrimination, and as such underlies the basic feature of contemporary legal systems: their tolerant, democratic, individualistic character. The discovery was to a large extent due to Christianity. A conviction about the fundamental equality of all human beings is expressed in many passages of the New Testament, such as in St Paul's Letter to Galatians (3, 28): 'There is neither Jew nor Gentile, neither slave nor free, nor is there male and female, for you are all one in Christ Jesus.' Christianity also emphasized that the individual stands above the state. These moral insights were later 'rediscovered' or 'taken over' in secular thought. They were expressed in a clear, though still imperfect, form in *The Declaration of the Rights of Man and of the Citizen* from 1789, which provided that 'men are born and remain free and equal in rights' (Art. I) and that 'the goal of any political association is the conservation of the natural and imprescriptible rights of man: liberty, property, safety and resistance against oppression' (Art. II). The expression was imperfect, because it still allowed 'social distinctions' (though only if they were founded on the common good (cf. Art. I)), said nothing about the rights of women or the abolition of slavery, and was not concerned with the issue of material equality.

I wrote above about the individualistic, egalitarian character of contemporary legal systems. It bears emphasis that such systems are a true novelty in history. In ancient thought and tradition an individual was considered to be subordinated to a state; he had no right to oppose the claims of the state. Even if he lived in a democratic state (such as Athens), his legal situation was little different. This was tacitly admitted by Pericles in his famous *Funeral Oration*, invoked by Thucidydes in his *Peloponnesian War*. Pericles declares that private life is respected in Athens, but adds several lines later that the individual who is uninterested in public affairs is regarded not as passive, but as useless. Thus, what may have looked like political rights (for instance, a citizen's 'right' to participate in collective decisionmaking) were therefore more akin to duties: the citizen's participation in public life was not a matter of personal choice; he was expected and at least socially obliged to participate in it. Furthermore, this participation – and its most important manifestation, the much vaunted *isegoria/parrhesia*, or freedom to speak in public and to be heard – involved dangers: if a citizen proposed a statute which proved to be inconsistent with the existing law or was deemed harmful to democracy, then he could be severely punished (by fine or loss of honour – *atymia*). Accordingly, political freedom is a misleading term as it refers to the ancient (republican) variant of this notion: it was a duty rather than a freedom. One should therefore be careful not to consider *isonomia* (equality before the law/equality of rights) and *isegoria/parrhesia* as similar to the terms 'equality before the law' and 'freedom of speech' in contemporary liberal democracies. The character of Greek political activity was basically determined by the above mentioned conviction that the state has a higher value than the individual; in this context one should therefore speak about the *collectivist justification* of political 'rights'. The problem of the individual's subordination to the state in the ancient world was insightfully analysed by the nineteenth-century French historian Fustel de Coulanges in his classic work *The Ancient City*. He emphasized that in the ancient states individual liberty was very limited, even in the otherwise enlightened Athenian democracy: not only did the 'body' of the citizen belong to the state (there was a duty of long military service, a duty of marriage; a citizen's fortune was to a large extent at the disposal of the state) but so did his 'soul':

> Liberty of thought in regard to the state religion was absolutely unknown among the ancients ... The ancients ... knew neither liberty in private life, liberty in education, nor religious liberty. The human person counted for very little against that holy and almost divine authority which was called country or the state ... The dangerous maxim that the safety of the state is supreme law was the work of antiquity ... To have political rights, to vote, to name magistrates, to have the privilege of being archon – this was called liberty. The ancients, especially the Greeks, always exaggerated the rights of society. This was largely due, doubtless, to the sacred and religious character with which society was clothed in the beginning. (de Coulanges 1882: 296, 297–8)

As mentioned, in the Athenian *polis* political activity was a duty. But, as de Coulanges aptly remarked, individuals may have had an additional motivation, aside from the fear of sanction for absenteeism, to engage in political activity – a motivation connected with the absence of individual rights: political activity was the only way to protect their own individual interests. One can therefore view extensive political freedom as a compensation for the lack of private – 'true' (as de Coulanges calls it) – freedom. Such freedom provided the best guarantee of safety and dignity in the absence of individual rights: '[given that] the collective sovereign was so omnipotent, a man could be nothing unless he was a part of it ... He wished to possess political rights, not in order to enjoy true liberty but to have at least what might take its place' (de Coulanges 1882: 438). Further analyses of de Coulanges provide an additional argument for what I have written above; in his view, the force which reversed the 'axiological' relations between the individual and the state/society/family was Christianity, which discovered the infinite value of each individual human being. Its contrast with the religion of the ancient city was enormous. In the old domestic religion (the ancestral one, the earliest form of religion in the ancient city), 'the family was the true body of which the individual was but an inseparable member ... The new religion [Christianity – WZ] recognized in [the] individual complete liberty and entire personal independence and was not in the least opposed to separating him from the family' (de Coulanges 1882: 147). It should be added that domestic religion was not the only form to have this closed character; civic religion (for example, that of the mature Greek *polis*) also placed sharp barriers between citizens and strangers. De Coulanges made an interesting observation in this context: 'It is not surprising that the ancient republics almost all permitted a convict to escape death by flight. Exile did not seem to be a milder punishment than death. The

Roman jurists called it capital punishment' (de Coulanges 1882: 207). He develops his claim about the revolutionary character of Christianity in the following way: 'If we bear in mind how far the [ancient –WZ] city, in the name of its sacred character and religion, which was inherent in it, exercised an absolute empire, we shall see this new [Christian – WZ] principle was the source whence individual liberty flowed' (de Coulanges 1882: 527). Man's conscience became free: 'in what related to his soul, he was bound only to God' (de Coulanges 1882: 527). Man's duties to his state/society/family were still appreciated but began to be deemed inferior to his duties to God and to other people (irrespective of their race, sex and ethnicity).

By way of a digression, which may be of interest, let me briefly present a different account of the process of individualization (that is, the gradual liberation of human beings from the domination of the state/society/family, and of the development of their individual egos), viz. the account proposed by the renowned nineteenth-century French sociologist Émile Durkheim (2011). According to Durkheim, whose perspective was more anthropological than historical, in the early stages of social evolution, individuals were part of a social group; their individuality was weakly developed, their identity was to a large extent common. Durkheim claimed that if individualism were deeply embedded in human nature, it would be difficult to understand why human beings so easily yielded to the despotic chiefs; if it is assumed that human beings are, initially, a part of a group, which exerts almost despotic power over them, it becomes no longer surprising that they may be willing to submit to a person who has accumulated great power, since this person can be viewed as representing a group (cf. Durkheim 2011: 249). He believed that the process of the crystallization of individuality was strictly connected with the gradual increase of division of labour (which, in turn, was caused by the increase in population – its quantity and density – and the resulting competition between individuals; the function of the division of labour was to decrease this competition and the resulting social conflicts). Another part of his theory was that human beings were not originally *solely* egoistic: altruism was a part of their dispositional framework. Thus, according to Durkheim, we should reject two myths: the myth of primitive individualism (leading to the erroneous belief that collective life evolved from individual life), and the myth of primitive egoism (the readiness with which an individual sacrifices himself for the group is incompatible with it; egoism existed but was from the very beginning accompanied by (group) altruism). Durkheim had certainly exaggerated the extent of primitive societies' collectivism: individual egos were arguably more developed at this time than he thought (which seems also to be implied by the theory of natural selection, which assumes that the basic unit of selection is the individual, not the group). But his account remains inspiring and apt insofar as it is viewed as providing a counterbalance to those views which ascribe a similar degree of individualism to primitive and developed societies: this degree was much lower in primitive societies.

To return to the main discussion: what more general conclusions flow from the above considerations on the differences between the ideological basis of primitive egalitarianism and that of contemporary egalitarianism? The following seems to be of particular importance: if, as I have argued, the egalitarian ideology of contemporary liberal democracies *is not* an expression of human nature, then this political form should be regarded as inherently fragile (a telling illustration of the unreliability of human natural moral tendencies is that human beings were able to tolerate slavery for the greater part of human history; slavery disappeared in Western Europe very late: for example, Great Britain banned the slave trade only in 1807; France banned it twice, in 1794 and 1848, because Napoleon I made it legal again in 1802; the United States abolished it in 1865). Thus, the fact that human beings have managed to create this political form is a kind of anthropological miracle. Accordingly, there is a strong tension between biological evolution and (the contemporary form of) democracy: the former assumes that human beings are endowed with hierarchical propensities which may give rise only to 'primitive egalitarianism', while contemporary liberal democracy is a political system based on the idea of moral equality and the fundamental rights of all human beings irrespective of their individual qualities. It is worth noting, however, that the view of human nature as doubly ambivalent may, at the same time as showing the 'unnaturalness' of liberal democracy, provide its justification. Such justification is based on the observation that liberal democracy can be viewed as an 'institutionalized distrust' towards human beings: no individual human being is so trustworthy as to be vested with absolute power over other people, and even democratically chosen power should be limited by various systems of checks and balances and by the requirement of respect for fundamental rights (cf. Sztompka 2007). Accordingly, democracy is justified if mistrust of human nature is justified, that is, if the nonoptimistic picture of human nature is apt. Evolutionary theory, as I have argued, supports precisely such a picture – a picture of human nature as doubly ambivalent.

4. MORE SPECIFIC DIRECTIONS OF PROGRESS

As I have argued, progress in law consisted in evolution from the rules expressive of evolutionary ethics to the rules of genuine ethics as the result of moral discoveries. Most of the (progressive) changes in law can be justified by the fundamental moral discovery made by human beings – the discovery of the equal and infinite (or at least very great) moral value (that is, dignity) of each human being. However, the process which led to the full implementation of this discovery in law was long, arduous, gradual, and nonlinear: step by step, with much backward as well as forward movement, various forms of arbitrary differential treatment of human beings were removed; as a final result of this process, the doctrine of moral egalitarianism has fully established itself (at least in Western legal systems). In this section I shall present, in a very broad outline, various strands of this process. Initially, however, I shall make two general remarks.

First, it seems that the (doubly) ambivalent – imperfectly moral – nature of human beings has, somewhat paradoxically, been a greater obstacle to moral and legal progress than a deeply flawed nature would have been, because the former tended to give rise to poor substitutes of genuine ethics, viz. variants of evolutionary ethics which may have come to be regarded as genuine ethics.

Second, one should stress that law was rarely a simple and accurate reflection of evolutionary ethics. Let me illustrate this claim with some examples from the history of family law. Fustel de Coulanges asserted that the ancient family was 'a religious rather than natural association' and that although religion 'did not create the family ... certainly it gave the family its rules; and hence it comes that the constitution of the ancient family was so different from what it would have been if it had owed its foundation to natural affection' (de Coulanges 1882: 52). He may have exaggerated this point: the very religion itself (the cult of ancestors – of *Manes*, in the Roman civilization) appears to be an expression of natural affection. But he was certainly right in claiming (though, of course, he did not use these words) that the ancient rules were not a *simple* reflection of the logic of kin altruism. For instance, the system of relationship based upon blood ties (the so-called *cognatio*) was absent in the early stages of Roman civilization: the dominant system was *agnatio*, based on *potestas* (power) of one father, and two persons were *agnati* if they were related (by nature or by law, that is, through adoption) to the same father. To determine a relationship based on *agnatio* one therefore took into account only the male line. Furthermore, in Roman law, (married) women could not inherit and inheritance could pass, in accordance with the system of *agnatio*, only to the male relatives in the male lines. The exclusion of women and relatives in the female line (*cognates* who are not *agnates*) is, of course, contrary to kin altruism. It is worth emphasizing, however, that the departure of this system from the 'logic of natural affection' was only partial: it was, ultimately, still based on blood relationships, albeit 'truncated' ones – one was not related to the relatives of one's mother (though it may be interesting to note that from the standpoint of evolutionary theory the reverse form of partiality would be more understandable, because *mater simper certa est*). But, interestingly, one can try to explain this departure from the logic of natural affection by noticing that these rules may be a result of opposite *male* evolutionary proclivities: the fear of women's freedom and the consequent willingness to subordinate women. The institution of adoption seems to be another departure from the logic of natural affection. This institution, however, was usually treated as a last resort (perhaps with the exception of Roman civilization, where it was extremely popular). *The Laws of Manu*, for instance, provided that 'he to whom nature has denied a son can adopt one, so that the funeral ceremonies may not cease' (quoted after de Coulanges 1882: 68). To conclude: hardly any legal rule, including rules of primitive legal systems, can be viewed as a simple reflection or expression of our biological propensities, as an exact correlate; propensities are always or usually mediated by cultural patterns and symbols, which may distort their origin. However, the origin is often sufficiently visible so that one could regard a given legal rule as reflecting evolutionary ethics, and consequently could meaningfully speak about the progressive tendencies in law, from evolutionary ethics to genuine ethics. In the remainder of this chapter I shall describe several tendencies of this kind.

4.1 The Disappearance of Self-Help and of Group Responsibility

The crucial component of early legal systems was the institution of self-help (bloody revenge), in which the victim (direct or indirect) could, on his own or with the help of others, without invoking the apparatus of the state (if it existed at all), violently punish a person who had injured him or his kin. This institution can be viewed as an expression of our evolutionarily shaped neutral and moral tendencies: the emotion of anger (leading to the desire of vengeance), kin altruism, and reciprocal altruism. Anger (indignation) is a proper response to the violations of basic human values (life, health, physical integrity) but, in its primitive (evolutionary) form, it tends to overstep the boundaries of moral permissibility: it often leads to revengeful actions which are disproportionate to the sustained evil. However, in the early stages of the development of law (and of morality), actions caused by anger were not conceived in this way (that is, as overstepping the boundaries of morally permissible actions); they were regarded, even in their violent forms, as morally permissible or even obligatory. Legal rules which accepted them were therefore a direct expression of the second ambivalence of human nature (that is, of the distortion of our evolutionarily shaped moral or neutral tendencies). It is interesting to trace the differing attitudes to this institution in the Old Testament. It is accepted or even required in the Book of Numbers (35: 19, 31): 'The avenger of blood is the one who shall put the murderer to death; when they meet, the avenger of blood shall execute the sentence … you shall accept no ransom for the life of a murderer who is subject to the death penalty; a murderer must be put to death.' But in the Book of Leviticus (19: 18), we read that 'you shall not take vengeance or bear a grudge against any of your people, but you shall love your neighbour as yourself'. Of course, it took a long time to overcome this institution, which especially plagued medieval societies, leading to the so-called private wars.

Bloody revenge and self-help are connected with another element of the primitive (evolutionarily shaped) sense of justice: its, so to say, 'dispersed' character. It was not sensitive, or was not sufficiently sensitive, to the *individual* character of responsibility; the dominant form of responsibility was *group* (*collective*), that is, one could extend the responsibility of a crime's perpetrator to the members of the group to which the perpetrator of the crime belonged (for example, to his family). Because the perpetrator did not have to be alive for such an extension to be possible, group responsibility was at the same time, as one might call it, 'intergenerational'. The fact that responsibility initially had a group character can be at least partly explained by appealing to kin and group altruism and the related fact (emphasized or overemphasized by Durkheim) that individuality was not developed in the early stages of human history. As noted by Katarzyna Sójka-Zielińska (2000: 23), the evolution of the character of responsibility can be seen in the Old Testament, for instance: group responsibility is required in the Book of Numbers, but in the Book of Deuteronomy (24: 16) it is firmly rejected: 'Parents shall not be put to death for their children, nor shall children be put to death for their parents; only for their own crimes may persons be put to death.'

4.2 The Trend towards Proportionality in Punishing

The law of the talion (*lex talionis*), that is, the law of retaliation – typical of early legal systems – requires that the perpetrator of a crime be punished in such a way that his injuries sustained as a result of the punishment should be the same as (equal to) those which he imposed on the victim, or (if literal sameness of the crime and the punishment is not possible) should somehow 'reflect' or 'mirror' the crime. *Lex talionis* is a moral rule but constitutes an expression of the second ambivalence of human nature, viz. of primitive, evolutionarily shaped moral tendencies – reciprocal altruism and anger (indignation) giving rise to the desire for revenge. However, as is rightly emphasized by legal historians, *lex talionis*, owing to an element of 'equilibrium' built into it, can be viewed as a progression as compared with self-help (which, by its nature, leads to uncontrolled punishment). It therefore constitutes a step towards institutionalized punishment. One can therefore say that even though *lex talionis* is still an expression of evolutionary ethics (because it admits of a primitive retaliation), it is a *limited* expression, because the extent of revenge is strictly circumscribed. But it must be admitted that *lex talionis* is the simplest, most primitive expression of the sense of (retributive) justice, because proportionality, which is built into the concept of justice, appears here only, so to say, as a side effect. Let me explain. The principle of proportionality in punishment means equality in the *ratios* of severity of punishment to severity of crime. In order to build a system of proportional punishments, one must have, of course, a pattern of adequate punishment for at least one crime, which could serve as a basis of evaluation (comparison) as to whether other crimes are punished proportionately. Now, *lex talionis* does lead to a proportionate system of punishment, but its point of departure is not concern with *proportionality of the whole system of punishment*, but rather the justice – adequacy – of punishment for each concrete type of crime, viewed as if separate from other crimes. Equality in the ratios of crime and punishment appears here only as a side effect. This is the first reason – one may call it 'formal' – why the system of punishments based on *lex talionis* is primitive: it attests a rather low level of abstract moral thinking. The second reason is that it does not allow the introduction of punishments that are less severe than the crime, for example with the intention of resocializing the perpetrator (though in favour of *lex talionis* it must be said that the punishment cannot be more severe either); its inevitable consequence is, therefore, cruelty.

It may be interesting to invoke some historical facts. *Lex talionis* was introduced to the codes of the ancient East, such as the Code of

Hammurabi and the Old Testament. The Old Testament's early books admit unlimited vengeance: 'Then the Lord said to him, "Not so! – Whoever kills Cain will suffer a sevenfold vengeance"' (Book of Genesis 4: 15) ('sevenfold' is to be taken metaphorically as meaning 'unlimited'). But in later books one reads: 'If any harm follows, then you shall give life for life, eye for eye, tooth for tooth, hand for hand, foot for foot, burn for burn, wound for wound, stripe for stripe' (Book of Exodus 21: 23–4); 'Anyone who kills a human being shall be put to death. Anyone who kills an animal shall make restitution for it, life for life. Anyone who maims another shall suffer the same injury in return: fracture for fracture, eye for eye, tooth for tooth; the injury inflicted is the injury to be suffered' (Book of Leviticus 24: 17–20) (cf. also Book of Deuteronomy 19: 16–21). The Old Testament was sometimes even more severe than the Code of Hammurabi; for instance, while the latter provided cutting the hand as a punishment for hitting one's father, the former, infringing on the law of retaliation, provided that 'whoever strikes their father or mother shall be put to death … Whoever curses their father or mother shall be put to death' (Book of Exodus 21: 15, 17; and similarly in Book of Leviticus 20: 9; it is worth noticing, however, that the Old Testament protected not only fathers but also mothers). But in other cases it was the Code of Hammurabi which manifested special severity in the application of *lex talionis*: it provided, for instance, that the punishment for killing a woman was killing one of the perpetrator's daughters. It is interesting to note that the severe (and yet on the other hand progressive) *lex talionis* was unknown to the benign codes of Sumer, earlier than Hammurabi. These mainly provided penalties in terms of fines rather than physical punishments.

4.3 The Elimination of Cruel Punishments

Over the course of history, motivational incentives used by the legislator underwent a substantial change, viz. the role of cruel punishments steadily diminished. This was, however, an arduous and nonlinear process.

I shall start my (selective) description of this process with the laws of Athens introduced by Draco in the seventh century BC. These laws were notoriously severe ('draconian') – they provided for punishment by death for a large number of crimes. When Draco was asked why he had introduced such severe laws, he is said to have replied that even lesser crimes deserve to be punished by death, and for greater crimes he could find no more severe punishment than death (cf. Kuryłowicz 2006: 137). Even the otherwise humanitarian Roman law provided very cruel punishments, such as qualified capital punishment (*damnatio ad bestiae* – throwing the convict to wild animals; crucifixion; *poena cullei* – drowning of the convict sewn with wild animals in a bag, or burning alive); books 47 and 48 of *Digesta* (the Emperor Justinian's legal code), in which these punishments were described, were called 'terrible books' (*libri terribiles*). In Roman civil law, the situation of the insolvent debtor was initially very dramatic. According to *Lex duodecim tabularum* (451 BC), if no one would pay the debt of an insolvent debtor, his creditors could sell him into slavery and even kill and dismember him, dividing parts of his body among themselves in proportion to the amount of their claims. However, such severe rules in contract law disappeared from the legal codes at quite an early stage: there was an evolution from personal liability to property liability (and also a separation of civil law from criminal law: the above mentioned rule from *Lex duodecim tabularum* shows that no clear distinction was made between a theft and a failure to pay off a debt, and neither was regarded as a public crime). In later legal systems, penalties had a cruel character as well. Many of them involved mutilation or degradation, for example pillorying or whipping, and capital punishment was often inflicted in a barbarous way, for example by using such torture devices as the breaking wheel or by burying the person alive. It may be interesting to note, as an illustration of the nonlinearity of the process through which the law became more humanitarian, that modern legal systems, which came into being as a result of the development of the absolutist state, were often less humanitarian than the earlier, medieval ones. For instance, the German criminal code from 1532 (*Constitutio Criminalis Carolina*), while progressive insofar as it explicitly recognized the subjective attitude of the perpetrator – *dolus* or *culpa* – as the basis of legal responsibility, was (in)famous for its system of cruel punishments. This system was based on two assumptions: that an important goal of punishment is deterrence, and that the penalties which 'reflect' or 'mirror' a type of crime are at the same time just and the most effective in terms of deterrence (hence the system embraced a diversified system of penalties – for instance, it provided eight types of death penalty, viz. by drowning, hanging, burying alive, burning alive, impaling, quartering, breaking on the wheel, and decapitation). This is not the only way in which *Constitutio Criminalis Carolina* infringed upon the principle of human dignity. Apart from providing a system of cruel punishments, it also allowed analogical reasoning in criminal cases and extraordinary (that is, not introduced explicitly in the code) penalties. Accordingly, it did not respect two principles of criminal law which are contemporarily regarded as fundamental, viz. *nullum crimen sine lege* and *nulla poena sine lege* (though it should be added that the provision about extraordinary punishments was often used in a humanitarian spirit, in order to avoid using the harsh 'ordinary' punishments).

Little progress can be seen over the two centuries that follow. The Bavarian Criminal Code, *Codex Bavarius Criminalis* (1751), provided, for instance, the penalty of burning alive for 'physical intercourse with the devil' and host desecration (cf. Dziadzio, Malec 1997). The Austrian Criminal Code from 1768, *Constitutio Criminalis Theresiana*, was almost equally backward: it admitted analogical reasoning in criminal cases, extraordinary punishments, inequality before criminal law (degrading penalties could not be inflicted on noblemen), a system of cruel penalties, and the death penalty for blasphemy and witchcraft. It therefore comes as no surprise that it was called *Nemesis Theresiana*. Cruelty was also widespread at the level of legal process. Torture was a frequent method of interrogation of the accused during the so-called inquisitorial process.

The turning point in the process of elimination of the cruel punishments involving degradation and mutilation was the so-called humanitarian revolution of the eighteenth century, involving such thinkers as Christian Thomasus, Jacques Pierre Brissot, Cesare Beccaria, Voltaire, Gaetano Filangieri, and many others (cf., for example, Dziadzio 2008: 150–1). Their postulates were motivated by their belief in the dignity of human beings, which, as they stressed, is not respected if human beings' freedom from the arbitrary interventions of the state power is not guaranteed. Accordingly, they were strongly opposed to the arbitrariness of judicial decisions; they required that the criminal law system be based on such principles of legalism as *nulla crimen sine lege* and *nulla poena sine lege*, as well as the principle *nulla crimen sine culpa* (emphasizing the subjective side of a crime), and were also against using analogical reasoning in criminal processes. Furthermore, they believed in the equality of all individuals before criminal law: the sense they gave to this notion was not purely formal (that of consistent application of rules) but also moral, according to which rules themselves could not introduce any differentiation of individuals on the basis of morally irrelevant factors. This was a true revolution, because, for the largest part of its history, law provided different punishments for the same crimes depending on the social status of the perpetrator and the victim: the higher the place a given person occupied in the social hierarchy, the milder the punishment he sustained if he committed a crime, and the greater the punishment inflicted for committing a crime against him. The rich or the noble could also pay a certain amount of money to avoid corporal punishment.

Furthermore, since the 'humanitarians' believed that only socially harmful actions may be deemed crimes, they also opposed the penalization of religious offences, of suicide, of witchcraft; they propagated the ideal of religious tolerance. They also postulated the introduction of limitation periods for the prosecution of crimes, condemned public executions, and defended the utilitarian justification of punishment (since, as they claimed, retributive justification is often just an expression of the desire for revenge). Furthermore, many of them (for example, Beccaria) rejected capital punishment, arguing either that it is cruel (and teaches cruelty) or that it has very limited deterrent power. For similar reasons, they rejected the use of penalties involving degradation or mutilation. They also criticized the penalty of property confiscation, which they viewed as a relic of group responsibility (property confiscation affects not only the perpetrator of a crime but also his family). However, they were not against compulsory work; they believed in its usefulness, and especially its deterrent power. As far as criminal legal procedure is concerned, they postulated introducing the presumption of innocence, abolishing torture as a method of extracting confessions, and providing the right to defence to the accused – who was to become a subject of the procedure, not merely an object (as was the case in the inquisitorial procedure). Many postulates of the humanitarian doctrine were embodied in criminal law codes. For instance, the Tuscan criminal code *Constitutio Criminalis Leopoldina* (1786) abolished capital punishment and degrading penalties; the Austrian Code *Costitutio Criminalis Josephina* (1787) introduced the principle of *nullum crimen sine lege*, abolished arbitrary penalties (and thereby accepted the principle *nulla poena sine lege*), and did not penalize witchcraft; the presumption of innocence was provided by the *Declaration of the Rights of Man and Citizen* (1789); and the Decrees of the French *Constituante* (from 1789) abolished torture and gave the accused the right of defence.

However, one cannot speak of the full triumph of the humanitarian doctrine in the historical epoch in which it was proposed. In *Constitutio Criminalis Josephina* one can find such penalties as stigmatizing a perpetrator by branding his face, or ship pulling on the Danube (*Schiffziehen*). The criminal code of Napoleon (from 1810) provided capital punishment for many crimes (and even qualified punishment for patricide – cutting off the palm of a perpetrator's right hand before execution; it was repealed in 1832), confiscation of property, civil death (until 1854), stigmatizing a convict by branding signs on his body (until 1854), and pillory (until 1848). In general, as noted by Katarzyna Sójka Zielińska (1997: 332), corporal penalties of mutilation disappeared from European codes the earliest – at the beginning of the nineteenth century (nonmutilating corporal penalties, such as whipping, were retained for a longer period – in the German states until the middle of the nineteenth century, in Russia until 1863, and in Austria until 1867). Nonetheless, as we can see, the path to full victory of humanitarian ideals was long indeed. It should also be stressed that the humanitarian revolution did not eliminate all injustices from the law. For instance, women did not have voting rights, homosexual people were prosecuted, and interracial marriages were prohibited in many legal systems.

4.4 The Transition from Legal Moralism to Legal Liberalism

Another tendency in the evolution of the content of criminal law consists in its passing from legal moralism to legal liberalism. According to the former view, the law may (or even should) enforce also those moral rules which do not serve the cause of protecting other people from harm (this view justifies, for example, *leges sumptuariae* – against luxury, introduced by many lawgivers in the past, from Solon, through Octavian Augustus, to Calvin; or laws against religious or sexual offences). According to the latter view, the law may not enforce rules which serve the realization of some moral ideal not directly connected to the protection of other people from harm. Two elements of this transition are worth stressing: the reversal of the hierarchy of crimes (including the desacralization of law), and the depenalization of some types of sexual behaviour.

In the course of the development of criminal law, the hierarchy of crimes substantially changed and the very category of 'crime' broadened. Initially, state treason, desertion from a military, and violation of religious rules (for example, blasphemy, witchcraft, false accusations and testimony, perjury) were considered to be the most serious crimes (even in enlightened Athens the smallest violations of religious ceremonies were harshly punished, often by death). They were in fact treated as crimes in the strict sense (*crimina publica*), that is, prosecuted by the state (cf. Durkheim 2011: 122–3). At this stage, punishment had a sacral character to a great extent: its main purpose was to propitiate the deity offended by, for example, false testimony, false accusation or perjury (the crimes that are mentioned in the first lines of the Code of Hammurabi). In general, the first laws were part of religion: they were viewed as having been created or revealed by deities. Over time, crimes against individuals – against their basic rights – came to be treated as equally serious, or even more serious, than crimes against the state or against religion; they began, in fact, to be regarded as crimes in the strict sense (*crimina publica*).

Initially, law penalized many types of sexual behaviour, regarding them as 'perverted' or 'unnatural'. For instance, homosexuality was penalized by the majority legal systems – from the Old Testament (Book of Leviticus Ch. 20), through *Constitutio Criminalis Carolina* (1532), to many twentieth-century legal codes. Often the codes penalized only male homosexuality, but, for instance, *Constitutio Criminalis Carolina* treated male and female homosexuality symmetrically: both 'crimes' were punishable by death (burning). The penalization was repealed in France in 1791 and in Turkey in 1858, but in Canada as late as 1959, in England and Wales in 1967, in Ireland in 1993, and in the USA in 2003. As mentioned previously, the criminalization of homosexuality was to a large extent caused by the process called 'moralization of disgust', that is, the conversion of aversions (engendered by disgust) into disvalues, and subsequently into rules prohibiting the 'disgusting' conduct. The same process may have played a role in the condemnation of interracial marriages, which were legalized in the USA only in 1967, when the last antimiscegenation law was repealed. It is worth noting that one can treat the antimiscegenation laws, as well as, for instance, enforced public segregation (abolished in the USA only in 1964, with the Civil Rights Act), as manifestations of tribal thinking.

One can see the evolution from legal moralism to legal liberalism also in the changing approaches to the institution of marriage. Initially, marriage was obligatory: celibacy was severely punished, with the Spartan laws established by Lycurgus providing that an unmarried man lost his right of citizenship, for example. This kind of regulation flowed from the already mentioned fact that, in ancient times, man belonged more to the family and the state than to himself; it was his duty to continue the domestic religion and to take care of the worship of his ancestors; and since celibacy raised the danger of ending this cult, it was regarded, as de Coulanges put it, as 'impiety' – 'one who did not marry put the happiness of the *manes* of the family in peril, and misfortune: he himself would receive no worship after his death' (de Coulanges 1882: 63). Such regulations were an expression of family and tribal ethics, and, at a deeper level, of kin and group altruism.

4.5 The Improvement of Women's Legal Status

Over time, women's legal status improved. For centuries, the status was an inferior one: women were regarded as the weaker sex not only physically but also mentally. The Latin term used by medieval lawyers to describe this inferiority was *infirmitas sexus et levitas animi*, describing the '(physical) weakness of sex and the fickleness/lightness of soul' from which women were believed to suffer. Accordingly, their legal capacity, in various branches of civil law (for example, the law of inheritance or contract law), was strongly limited. In one of the oldest written legal codes – the Code of Hammurabi – a woman was regarded, in some contexts, as the property of her husband: a debtor could pay his debt by passing his wife (as well as his children) to his creditor. Nor could women inherit. However, despite its patriarchal spirit, a woman's position within this code was, comparatively, good: she could leave her husband and even take her dowry if he gravely insulted her, and she could go to the house of another man if her husband became a war prisoner and she was without means of living (cf. Kuryłowicz 2006: 85). The position of many women was even better in the earlier codes of the ancient East (which illustrates the rather obvious truth that the progress in law was not linear). For instance, in the Code of Lipit-Ishtar (1870–1860 BC) the position of a wife was protected: a husband was obliged to support a blind or paralyzed wife, even if he had taken a second wife as a result of the first wife's illness, and if a husband divorced his wife because of a love affair with a 'harlot', he could not marry the second woman (cf. Kuryłowicz 2006: 88). On the other hand, women's status was especially low in the Assyrian legal system: a woman – considered as a source of sin – could not appear in public without a veil on her face and a cover on her head, under threat of severe penalties; a wife could be killed with impunity by her husband if she was caught *in flagrante delicto* with her lover.

Marriage did not originally have a consensual character: the man was in fact buying his wife (or power over his wife) from her family (the woman was not asked for consent). However, in a relatively short space of time, the woman's consent became a necessary condition of the validity of marriage. For instance, in the Roman code *Lex duoedecim tabularum* (451 BC), the legal position of women was strengthened: marriage was made on *mutuus consensus et affectio maritalis* (mutual consent and affection). This does not change the fact, though, that in Roman law men had the dominant position in marriages. A husband was endowed with legal power over his wife, which power included his right to punish his wife (the so-called *correctio maritalis*). This inequality in the relationships between men and women did not change for the most part of human history (though, of course, they could be more or less unequal; for instance, the situation of women in ancient Greece was even worse than that in ancient Rome). Even in the Civil Code of Napoleon (1807), which was otherwise progressive (that is, in the areas of property and contract law), women were placed under the 'power of husband' (*puissance maritale*). The husband – *pater familias* – had immense power over his wife and children; for instance, a wife could not take any legal action without her husband's consent, and the husband could assert control over her social contacts and correspondence. A husband could also demand a divorce at any time, while a wife could demand it only when her husband kept a lover, against his wife's will, in their common, family house. Furthermore, women were deprived of parental power over their children: full power belonged to the father (in fact, France granted equal parental rights to both parents only in 1970). As far as relations between a husband and wife were concerned, the Napoleonic Code was extremely patriarchal and antiegalitarian. But, in point of fact, while no other nineteenth-century legal code was as patriarchal as the Napoleonic Code, nor did any other code provide equal rights for men and women in their personal (family) relationships.

Discrimination against women manifested itself especially acutely in the sexual sphere. The long penalization of adultery could have been mentioned (as an instance of legal moralism) in the context of my discussion of the transition from legal moralism and legal liberalism. However, a more interesting aspect of this penalization (to be discussed here) is that it was defined in terms of the woman's status: a necessary 'participant' in an adulterous affair was a married woman, not a married man (for example, Thomas Aquinas, in *Summa Theologiae* (I–II, q. 92) defined adultery as *concubitus cum uxore alieni* – sexual intercourse with a wife of another man). If a wife engaged in extramarital sex, she committed a crime against her husband, who had then the right to compensation from her family and/or the right to divorce. But if it was a husband who engaged in extramarital sex, he did not commit a crime against his wife; it could at best be a crime against her family (especially her father or brother). Accordingly, it can be said that the legal (and moral) duty of marital fidelity rested only on the wife, not on the husband. There were a few exceptions to this rule. For instance, *Constitutio Criminalis Josephina* (1787) defined adultery as carnal intercourse between a spouse (that is, a wife or husband) and some person (married or unmarried) other than his or her spouse. According to this code, the crime of adultery was prosecuted on complaint and the punishment – flogging or prison – was not inflicted if the harmed spouse – husband or wife – decided to forgive the adulteress or the adulterer. In general, however, adultery was, so to say, a female crime (defined according to the woman's status), and severely punished. The harshest punishments – indeed, death – were introduced by the codes of the ancient East. For instance, the Code of Hammurabi provided that the adulterous wife and her lover should be drowned and the Old Testament provided that they should be put to death (without specifying the type of punishment – though one may suppose, relying on knowledge of the customs of the Jewish society, that it was stoning). However, the Code of Hammurabi, unlike the Old Testament, provided that the punishment need not be inflicted if the husband forgave the adulterous wife (cf.

Kuryłowicz 2006: 124). Only in exceptional cases did discrimination in the law fall in favour of women. For instance, the penalty for killing a woman was often higher than for killing a man, since, as the argument of the time went (invoking the doctrine of *infirmitas sexus*), a woman, being physically weak, could not defend herself; the same doctrine was used to justify milder penalties for crimes if they were committed by women (both differences were abolished in the Italian cities in the Middle Ages).

The causes of discrimination against women were complex and differentiated (psychological, biological, sociological) but, from the standpoint of evolutionary theory, one cause should be emphasized: that is, men's fear of women's extensive freedom, above all freedom in the sexual sphere – a fear that was understandable (though, of course, not *ipso facto* justifiable) insofar as that freedom could put a man at risk of devoting his time and energy to raising children not his own. An important function of the limitations on women's freedom was therefore the reduction of paternal uncertainty. More precisely, one can say that the peculiarities of evolutionary sexual ethics, which express men's desire to control their wives' sexuality, were the result of two matters: (1) relatively high (as compared with other species) parental investment on the part of the husband, though of course still much lower than the investment of women (this high parental investment is caused by what is known as neoteny, or the prolonged period of childhood, with children born entirely helpless); (2) the uncertainty of paternity (caused, or rather sharpened, by the fact that women, in contrast with other species, do not show external signs of ovulation). These two facts make the possibility of adultery a serious threat to a woman's partner's evolutionary success because, as noted, it exposes him to the risk of unconsciously investing resources in another man's offspring. It is argued that a mental mechanism that evolved in men to reduce the risk of cuckoldry is their proclivity to possessiveness of their wives (or sexual partners), treating them as a 'chattel' (Wilson, Daly 1992). Its most obvious manifestation is sexual jealousy, which hypersensitizes men to any potential sign of a women's infidelity, and, when triggered, often results in violence. Women are almost never exposed to similar risks: it would be extremely rare for a woman to be unaware that she has reared another woman's child. Thus, it is only the man that can be a victim of a *fundamental* (from the viewpoint of biological fitness) deception: that of being manipulated into rearing children not his own, of making vain sacrifices to ensure the survival of his putative offspring. It is worth noting that the possibility of a woman involving a man in the upbringing of another man's children was invoked as a (misguided) justification of women's stricter marital duties. Thus, it can be said that adultery on the part of a woman was condemned because of its potential negative consequences for the putative father of any child born out of the adultery. But this biological motivation (more or less conscious) was often supplemented by a religious one. In the primitive religion (the cult of ancestors) it was believed that a child born of adultery cannot continue family worship, and adultery therefore violated the rules of religious purity; as noted by Fustel de Coulanges, adultery 'disturbed the order of birth' (de Coulanges 1882: 127), and thus undermined the worship of ancestors. In Christianity, in turn, adultery was viewed in the first place as a defilement of the institution of marriage.

To summarize, men's fear of female infidelity and of the fundamental deception, which resulted in possessive behaviour towards women, found its expression in the law, which provided severe punishment for unfaithful wives, treated adultery as a property violation, valued female chastity, recognized infidelity as an exculpatory provocation to violence, and allowed or even ordered various types of surgery (such as infibulation and clitoridectomy) aimed at decreasing women's capacity to experience sexual pleasure. One can therefore say that stronger moral and legal condemnation of women's infidelity is a direct expression of evolutionary ethics – of the evolutionarily determined value judgement that the greater blame, because of its negative consequences for the other side, is to be attributed to a wife's adultery.

4.6 The Appearance of Children's Rights and Equalization of the Rights of Marital and Extramarital Children

The legal status of children gradually improved over time (though the very notion of 'the rights of children' is a very recent achievement). There were at least three different types of immoral treatment of children which had to be overcome.

The first consisted in not treating them as full human beings deserving of respect and consideration. Initially, for instance, in *Lex duodecim tabularum*, the rights of the father – *pater familias* – over his children were enormous – they included *ius vitae ac necis* (the right to life and death), and the right to sell his children. In the later stages of the development of law, children's legal status improved but, generally, they were regarded as parents' property. It is interesting to note that the tendency to grant equal parental rights to both spouses (of which I wrote earlier in this chapter) was accompanied by the tendency to grant the state rights to intervene in family relationships with a view to protecting the interests of children.

The second type of treatment that needed to be overcome was treating children as adults in situations in which they ought not to be thus treated. For instance, the Napoleonic criminal code (1810) provided only two periods of legal responsibility: (1) a period of conditional responsibility (until the age of 16); (2) a period of unconditional responsibility (from the age of 16). According to this system even a child could be responsible for a criminal action (if he or she acted with 'due discernment'); the three-period system dominant in other European states was accepted in France only in 1912 (the first period – of unconditional nonresponsibility – lasted until the age of 13 and the period of conditional responsibility from 13 to 18).

The third type of treatment to be overcome consisted in discrimination against extramarital children. For most of the history of law, the legal capacity of children born from extramarital relationships was limited (even in the Civil Code of Napoleon). But in the course of time they came to acquire the same rights (for example, the right of inheritance from a father, the right to take a father's name) as marital children. It is worth noting that discrimination against extramarital children cannot be regarded as an expression of our biological tendencies (unlike the harsh treatment of nonbiological children by their step-parents or killing weak or physically handicapped children, which, as previously mentioned, is said to be at least partly a result of what evolutionary biologists call 'discriminative parental solicitude'). Rather, it seems to have been a product of cultural processes. One may conjecture that the worsening of the status of extramarital children was caused (directly or as a side effect) by the religious and ethical doctrines which attached much importance to the institutions of marriage and family.

4.7 Individualistic and Social Welfarist Tendencies in Contract and Property Law

One manifestation of the individualistic tendency was the increasing significance of the autonomy of will in private law relations. This increasing significance had two dimensions, relating to the importance of the autonomy of will for the validity of contracts and the extent of its application. Regarding the first dimension, the crucial factor in assessing the validity of a contract was, in the early stages of the development of law, its form: if certain symbolic gestures were not observed the contract was deemed invalid, even if it conformed to the will of the parties. In the subsequent stages, the will became the crucial factor. As for the second dimension, the extent of the autonomy of will broadened because people were gradually gaining more freedom in the sphere of private law. For instance, initially, property rights were limited: since the land was regarded as belonging to a family, its current owner could not freely dispose of it. As Fustel de Coulanges expressed it: 'the living man was only the representation, for a few years, of a constant and immortal being – the family. He held the worship and the property only in trust; his right to them ceased with his life' (de Coulanges 1882: 107). This limitation can be viewed as an expression – or, rather, as a side effect – of kin altruism. In general, the direction of the development of private law was, so to say, antibiological and egalitarian. Property, which was initially regarded as belonging to a family or tribe, was taking on a more individualistic form and could be passed by will, though it must be stressed that the will (testamentary succession) came into law relatively late and initially in a limited form. For instance, Solon's laws allowed the owner to pass his property in a will only if he had no children; the son was still a 'necessary heir', and if the owner left only a daughter (who could not inherit on her own), he could nominate a heir only on condition that he should marry the daughter. Another peculiarity of inheritance law, which was preserved until the nineteenth century, was discrimination against the spouse: the spouse's 'place' in the nontestamentary succession was inferior, often behind that of distant cousins. One may see in the limitation of a spouse's succession right an unethical side effect of kin altruism (spouses are usually not genetically related to each other). It can be argued that the process of improving the spouse's position in nontestamentary succession was accelerated by Christianity, which placed spiritual ties above biological ones and thus contributed to the overcoming of 'family ethics'. Part of the same process was narrowing down the circle of nontestamentary successors; for instance, the circle no longer embraced the so-called *lachende Erben* (laughing heirs) – distant relatives of the testator, not related to him emotionally. This change can, again, be seen as overcoming or moving away from evolutionary ethics, an essential part of which is kin altruism. In general, freedom in the private law sphere has become broader. Various limitations, based on different legal statuses, have been abolished. The full development of these liberal and individualistic tendencies in property and contract law found its expression in the Civil Code of Napoleon, which provided a very strong right of private ownership and a very broad freedom of contract.

However, further developments in private law (from the second half of the nineteenth century onwards) proceeded in a different direction. The assumption of the absolute priority of individual interest over social interest was abandoned or at least weakened: freedom of contract and property rights were curtailed with a view to realizing social interests, especially protecting the weaker participants of social exchange. In several social doctrines (for example, in Leon Duguit's solidarism or in the Catholic Church's social doctrine), stress was put on the social function of property and on the owner's duty towards the society. Accordingly, the principle *violenti non fit iniuria* was weakened by the introduction of many exceptions, for instance, that the contract must be consistent with public order or the customs of honest commerce. These so-called general clauses implied that material justice is a necessary condition of the validity of contracts. These developments of private law, as well as the appearance of the so-called social rights, were propelled by concerns about the human dignity of the worst-off members of society and about social justice. One can therefore say that the circle of empathy has broadened once more, embracing also the less well-off members of society, such as poor people or people with disabilities (mental or physical). It seems plausible to maintain that a lack of empathy towards these less fortunate people was caused by emotions of disgust and contempt. The process of 'moralization' of these emotions could have engendered the pseudoethical conviction that the worst-off deserved their wretched social status.

5. GROUNDS FOR (RESTRAINED) OPTIMISM

There is an optimistic note in my considerations: they imply that there is progress in law, which is gradually (though not in a linear way) approaching the rules of genuine (impartial) ethics. But this optimism is restrained. Progress has been seen but one must remember that the law's 'default' option, to which it may return (and to which we keep on returning in our private lives), is a primitive type of ethics – evolutionary ethics. The achievements of this progress are therefore fragile, since genuine ethics does not become a part of our genotype. This view is radically different from more optimistic ones, such as that of the eminent Polish legal philosopher Leon Petrażycki (1959, 1960). He believed that the final stage of ethical evolution will be that of universal, rational love (benevolence), in which people will definitively go beyond 'tribal ethics' and will act morally in a spontaneous manner. They will not need to be motivated by punishment or reward. Law and morality will become superfluous. They have therefore a transitory character: they are needed only as long as human psychology is not adapted to the requirements of social life. Once egoism – individual and group – disappears, law and morality will no longer be necessary. The empirical assumption standing behind this utopian vision is 'Lamarckism' – the conviction that 'acquired traits' become part of our genotype and can be transmitted to subsequent generations. But neither element of this vision – Lamarckism or unrestrained optimism – can be reconciled with the evolutionary view of human nature.

3. Evolution, metaethics and the natural law

1. EVOLUTIONARY THEORY AND THE CONTENT OF LEGAL AND MORAL RULES

In the context of the question about the proper content of legal and moral rules, evolutionary theory can be used in several different ways. I shall argue that only two of these methods (Methods 5 and 6) are plausible.

Method 1: morally good = favouring the survival of the fittest

The first method consists in reasoning from the empirical statement that biological evolution proceeded in accordance with the principle of the survival and reproduction of the fittest to the normative conclusion that the main goal of legal and moral rules ought to be ensuring the survival and reproduction of the fittest. This method of applying evolutionary theory in the normative context is unacceptable for a number of reasons: (1) it rests on the 'naturalistic fallacy' described by George E. Moore (1903), that is, it erroneously identifies the predicate 'good' with the descriptive predicate (here the predicate 'contributing to the survival and reproduction of the fittest'), and thereby makes an illicit leap from the facts of evolution to values; (2) it leads to a normative conclusion entirely at odds with our basic moral intuitions (it would indeed be eccentric to claim that the survival and reproduction of the fittest ought to be the principal legal and ethical goal, or that mere survivability or leaving offspring exhausts the meaning of the term 'morally good'); (3) it is practically useless because, given the vagueness of the term 'fitness' when it is applied to human societies, it is close to impossible to ascertain which rules favour the survival and reproduction of the fittest (if we understand as 'fit' those who achieved some historical success, it may mean many different things; for example, one may argue that the Greeks were successful because they were creative and intelligent, the Romans because they were cruel and ruthless, the Christians because they were otherworldly and humble). It is dubious whether any serious thinker had ever used evolutionary theory in the normative context in that simplistic way. But it must be admitted that some form of the reasoning sketched above can be found in the writings of the representatives of so-called social Darwinism. Let me look more closely at the theory of Herbert Spencer, the best known of such representatives. Spencer argued for *laissez-faire* capitalism and, consequently, against state intervention in market processes (for example, against welfare programmes aimed at helping the poorest members of society). His argumentation rested on two highly questionable assumptions. The first asserts that the free market functions analogously to natural selection: it 'distributes' rewards and punishments in society according to individual merits, that is, those who are successful in the market enjoy the justified results of their capabilities and the unsuccessful (poor) suffer the justified results of their failings. The second is that the survival of those who have been successful in the socioeconomic struggle is more desirable than the survival of those who have been unsuccessful. Accordingly, he believed that the free market 'selects' the most valuable members of the society. In fact, he treated natural selection (in the strict biological sense) and 'selection' carried out by the competitive market as two instances of the same general law of nature, saying that 'an organism, placed in competition with members of its own species and in antagonism with members of other species, dwindles and gets killed off, or thrives and propagates, according as it is ill-endowed or well-endowed' (Spencer 1960: 106–7). Here are two suggestive quotations in which he criticizes the efforts to curb (by introducing the so-called laws of the poor) the beneficent (in his view) effects of the functioning of the market:

> Now that this truth [of Darwin's theory of evolution – WZ] is recognized by most cultivated people – now that the beneficent working of the survival of the fittest has been so impressed on them that, much more than people in the past times, they might be expected to hesitate before neutralizing its action – now more than ever before in the history of the world, are they doing all they can to further the survival of the unfittest! (Spencer 1960: 110)

And in similar vein:

> We must call those spurious philanthropists, who, to prevent present misery, would entail greater misery upon future generations. All defenders of a poor law [welfare] must, however, be classed among such. That rigorous necessity which, when allowed to act on them becomes so sharp a spur to the lazy … these paupers' friends would repeal, because of the wailings it here and there produces. Blind to the fact, that under the natural order of things society is constantly excreting its unhealthy, imprudent, slow, vacillating, faithless

> members, these unthinking though well-meaning men advocate an interference which not only stops the purifying process, but even increases the vitiation – absolutely encourages the multiplication of reckless and incompetent by offering them an unfailing provision and discourages the multiplication of the competent and provident by heightening the prospective difficulty of maintaining a family. And thus in their eagerness to prevent the really salutary sufferings that surround us, these sigh-wise and groan-foolish people bequeath to posterity a continually increasing curse … if they are sufficiently complete to live, they do live and it is well they should live. If they are not sufficiently complete to live, they die and it is best they should die. (Quotation from *The Social Statics*, in Spencer 1960: 113)

It is noteworthy that traces of a similar consideration of the fate of the worst-off members of society can also be found in Darwin's work *The Descent of Man*:

> We civilised men … do our utmost to check the process of elimination; we build asylums for the imbecile, and the sick; we institute poor-laws; and our medical men exert their utmost skill to save the life of everyone to the last moment … Thus the weak members of civilised society propagate their kind. No one who has attended to the breeding of domestic animals will doubt that this must be highly injurious to the race of man. (Darwin 1871: 90)

But, as rightly noted by Richard Hoftstadter, 'this was not characteristic of Darwin's moral sentiments … If there were, in Darwin's writings, texts for rugged individualists and imperialists, those who stood for social solidarity and fraternity could, however, match them text for text with some to spare' (Hoftstadter 1945: 91–2).

Method 2: morally good = consistent with the (morally acceptable) direction of evolution = favouring the all-round development of human beings

It should be stressed that Spencer's account of the relations between evolution and ethics, or, more generally, between facts and values, was far from being coherent. He understood these relations in a different way from the one sketched above (it seems that he did not clearly distinguish these two methods, or at least did not attempt to reconcile them with each other). This second method – which is also the second way of applying evolutionary theory in the normative context – is not based on giving a normative meaning to the claim about 'the survival of the fittest' (the basic law of biological evolution), but rather assigning to, or finding in, the very process of evolution a morally acceptable direction. In Spencer's writings, this takes the following form: (a) a theory of evolution reveals the direction of the living organisms' development; according to Spencer, this is the direction from incoherent homogeneity to coherent heterogeneity, that is, towards higher structural complexity, higher functional variety, and, consequently, greater length and hedonistic quality of life; (b) this direction is morally good; (c) therefore we ought to follow this direction.

There are three problems with this reasoning. The first one is empirical: Darwinian evolutionary theory does not provide any grounds to believe that evolution has any direction, let alone a direction towards ethical goodness. So part (a) of the above reasoning is indefensible. The second problem is conceptual. Spencer assumed (implicitly rather than explicitly) that the more developed life (with higher structural complexity and functional variety) is ethically better *because* it produces a greater amount of pleasure. Thus, he endorsed a version of hedonism (one could call it 'lifespan hedonism', as it puts stress on the length of life and its quality) which is exposed to the objection of the naturalistic fallacy, just like the claim that 'ethically good' means 'favouring the survival and reproduction of the fittest'. Accordingly, even if Spencer were right that evolution proceeds towards a state in which its 'products' (various living organisms) experience a greater amount of pleasure, it would still not prove that we ought to follow or favour the direction of evolution. In order to accept this conclusion, we would have to assume beforehand an additional – and implausible – claim that 'ethically good' means 'producing pleasure' (or, at least, that pleasure is a criterion of goodness). The third problem (connected with the previous one) is that invoking evolution in this reasoning is redundant, because Spencer's claim that the more a given organism is advanced in evolutionary development, the ethically better it is, does not have in his account a character of definition. Spencer seems to have started from the ethical *assumption* (without making any appeal to evolutionary theory) that 'morally good' means 'producing pleasure', or at least that pleasure is a criterion of goodness, and then made a dubious empirical claim (irrelevant to his ethical theory) that this criterion agrees with the direction of the evolutionary process.

Method 3: morally good = consistent with the direction of evolution, whatever it is

The third method of using evolutionary theory to determine the content of legal and moral rules consists in giving a normative meaning to the direction of evolution. This is, so to say, a formal approach, since it does not say *what the direction is*, but requires us to accept as ethically good *any* direction (and follow it), *whatever it is*; thus we should follow the direction determined by evolution *just because* it is the direction determined by evolution. This way, as rightly remarked by George E. Moore (1903: Chapter 2), is more interesting that the previous one because, were it successful (that is, if the direction of evolution were identified), it would give rise to a system which could rightly be called 'evolutionary ethics' (as mentioned, Method 2 introduces an additional normative premise, and thereby makes superfluous recourse to evolutionary theory). In this aspect it is similar to the first method, which could also be rightly called 'evolutionary ethics' (a fact which is not emphasized by Moore).

This method, however, encounters two serious difficulties. The first is that, as was already mentioned, evolution seems to be directionless (so the evolutionary ethics built in accordance with Method 3 cannot go beyond its formal stage). The second is that its central claim, viz. that a direction determined by evolution is ethically good *just because* it is determined by evolution, is entirely arbitrary: it is by no means clear why we should assign to this any moral weight. This claim could be accepted only in one case, viz. if we accepted the theistic account of evolution according to which evolution is God-directed (either 'from outside', as in the classical Christian theism, or 'from inside', as in Teilhard de Chardin's theory), or that biological evolution can be *identified* with God's activity, since God is nature (as in pantheism). But in this case, in turn, one would be less justified in dubbing this ethics 'evolutionary ethics'; a more proper name would be 'theistic ethics'.

Method 4: morally good = realizing the biological function of a given psychological/behavioural mechanism

The fourth method of deriving legal and moral norms from the facts of evolution – similar to the first, but slightly more subtle – consists in identifying a function of a given psychological/behavioural mechanism and interpreting this function normatively. Take, for instance, sexual intercourse. One might want to argue that, given that the function of sexual intercourse is reproduction, all kinds of non-reproductive sex are 'unnatural', and therefore morally wrong. But this conclusion is, of course, too rash, since it is by no means obvious that reproduction is the only or 'true' function of sexual intercourse: sexual intercourse may also strengthen interpersonal bonds or reduce aggression levels. Thus, this line of argumentation, besides being exposed to the objection of the naturalistic fallacy, is based on the false assumption that we know exactly the functions of various biological mechanisms. It also suffers from a different defect: since there are many unethical, natural mechanisms or propensities, we cannot derive from them any moral rules; we must know the rules *beforehand* in order to distinguish between moral and immoral mechanisms or propensities. Furthermore, many evolutionarily shaped propensities (for example, empathy and drive to obedience) may come into conflict with each other. In order to resolve conflicts between them (or their 'normative correlates'), one needs 'external' rules, that is, rules not derived from these propensities (since the only rule which might be thus derived – 'give priority to the stronger propensity' – is entirely implausible).

Method 5: morally good – only if (necessary condition) not requiring us to do what, in the light of evolutionary theory, proves to be impossible or prohibitively costly to do

The fifth method assumes that evolutionary theory can be used in a normative domain in a negative way – by narrowing down the scope of acceptable moral and legal rules. It is based on the assumption that evolutionary theory enables one to avoid pursuing goals that can hardly be realized given the 'boundary conditions' determined by human nature, and thereby to avoid the so-called moralistic fallacy: the mistaken conviction that 'what ought to be, can be'. In other words, it helps us respect the principle 'Ought implies Can' (*impossibilium nulla obligatio*), which requires us to be realistic in proposing legal and moral rules: not to demand anything which is either impossible to perform, or can be performed only with the utmost difficulty (at prohibitive costs). This – very promising and interesting – line of reasoning was thoroughly developed especially by the legal theorist Owen D. Jones (cf., for example, Jones 2005). He has argued that evolutionary theory (and, especially, evolutionary psychology) helps us understand the degree to which given predilections are hardwired into human nature, and thereby to determine what incentives are necessary to restrain these predilections or to channel them into cooperative behaviour. He proposed (as he called it) the 'law of law's leverage' – a conceptual tool inspired by evolutionary psychology to assess the comparative effectiveness of legal regulations. The name of this law is connected with the assumption that law exists to effect changes in human behaviour, thus being a kind of lever for moving human behaviour that 'depends on a behavioural model as a lever depends on a fulcrum' (Jones 1997: 167). The law says, roughly, that decreasing the frequency of behaviours by means of legal sanctions will be more difficult (that is, it will require higher sanctions) the more these behaviours tended, in ancestral environments, to increase the inclusive fitness of those who manifested them. The role of this law is important, because it 'can help us predict and explain the general features of the aggregated demand curves for different behaviors, and thereby helps us understand why some behaviors are less easily manipulated by law than are others' (Jones, Goldsmith 2005: 461). Jones noted that even though the law of law's leverage cannot be used either to precisely predict demand curves for law-relevant behaviours or to individualize a curve to a single person, it can offer general and useful insights into the ways in which law interacts with various behaviours. According to this law, for instance, the slope of the demand curve for adulterous behaviour will be comparatively steep and thus comparatively insensitive to legal sanctions (because, as evolutionary psychology teaches us, human beings are by nature moderately polygamous); the slope of the demand curve for jealous violence against potential rivals and partners, especially if the risk of sexual betrayal comes into play, will be much steeper for men than for women because of the different nature of male and female jealousy (sexual and emotional, respectively); given human beings' attachment to things, which is arguably a biological adaptation ('property instinct'), it may be safely supposed (and this supposition is confirmed by various unsuccessful utopian experiments in history) that all attempts at a durable abolition of private property are doomed to failure.

Method 6: evolutionary theory provides an indirect argument for ius-*naturalism*

The final method, to my knowledge unexplored so far, consists in making a link between evolutionary theory, metaethics and the controversy between the adherents of legal positivism and *ius*-naturalism (the natural law theories) about the nature of law. This proceeds in two steps. The first is that evolutionary theory supports metaethical (moral) non-naturalism, which is a version of metaethical (moral) realism. The second is that if one is a moral realist, then one should adopt the *ius*-naturalistic approach to the problem of the sources of legal normativity. In other words, if one believes that a certain system of moral norms is *true*, and that thereby 'moral Ought' exists, then one should not separate this 'Ought' from 'legal Ought'; rather, one should embed the latter in the former. In the remainder of this chapter I shall develop in detail this (undoubtedly controversial in both steps) line of argumentation. I shall start with a brief introduction to metaethics.

2. AN OVERVIEW OF METAETHICAL VIEWS

Metaethical views provide an answer to the question about the logical and ontological status of ethical rules (ethical sentences). One line of division among these views is between *moral non-naturalism* and *moral naturalism*. Moral non-naturalism assumes that ethical sentences can be true (it is thereby a variant of *moral realism*) and that they owe their truth value either to their being 'self-evident' or to non-natural facts/qualities/properties. Moral naturalism is an attempt to provide answers to metaethical questions without positing the existence of any non-natural facts or qualities. It appears in two versions: realist and antirealist. Realist moral naturalism asserts that moral facts exist and they are natural: they should be 'located' not in some non-natural sphere but in the world described by the empirical sciences. 'Hume's guillotine' and the objection of the naturalistic fallacy were directed precisely against this version of moral naturalism. Antirealist moral naturalism asserts that there are no moral facts whatsoever, not only non-natural ones. In its noncognitivist variant it denies that ethical sentences express beliefs; it assumes that moral properties which seem to exist 'in the world' are in fact just a projection of our emotions. Thus, even if moral properties may seem to be 'in the world', they are in fact 'appearances': they are generated by our emotional activity, which morally 'colourizes' the world. In its cognitivist variant, known as 'error theory' (proposed by John Mackie in 1977), antirealist moral naturalism assumes that ethical sentences express beliefs, that is, they possess truth values, but denies that these sentences are ever true; it thereby rejects the existence of moral facts or properties. Similar to error theory is moral fictionalism (Kalderon 2005; Joyce 2006), which assumes that ethical sentences express beliefs but are never true, and that these sentences are nevertheless useful but only if, knowing that they are false, we treat them in our everyday moral practice as if they were true. The difference between error theory and moral fictionalism is that while the former assumes that, in ordinary usage, people believe moral sentences to be true (and thereby are in error), the latter assumes that people use them (and should use them) fictively, that is, even though knowing that that they are not true, they use (and should use) them as if they were true. To summarize, we obtain the following classification of metaethical views:

(1) *Moral non-naturalism*, which is a variant of cognitivism (since it assumes that ethical sentences express beliefs, and thereby raise a

claim to truthfulness) and realism (since it assumes that some of these sentences are true).

(2) *Moral naturalism*:
   (a) realist (and thereby cognitivist)
   (b) antirealist and noncognitivist
   (c) antirealist and cognitivist (error theory, moral fictionalism).

As was mentioned above, realist moral naturalism is indefensible. The basic controversy is between moral non-naturalism and antirealist moral naturalism (in either of its versions – cognitivist or noncognitivist). Before I propose an evolutionary argument for moral non-naturalism, I shall present some other arguments for this view.

First, the tacit assumption of both variants of antirealist moral naturalism seems to be that for ethical sentences to have truth values, they must refer to some facts or properties – to some external reality. This assumption, however, is too strong. The sufficient condition for ascribing a truth value to a given sentence is that this sentence could be true in either of the two senses: that of corresponding to some external reality or that of being 'self-evidently' true.

Second, people engaged in ethical controversies have the irresistible impression of participating in *real* controversies, in which one party is right and the other is wrong, rather than in *apparent* ones, in which parties merely express their emotions and strive to influence other people's convictions and behaviour. This impression would have to be regarded as illusory if ethical sentences could not be the bearers of truth values. Antirealist moral naturalism in its cognitivist variant endeavours to explain this impression of objectivity by claiming that people are massively in error or use ethical language fictively. But this explanation is rather contrived. What is worse, it implies, contrary to most people's thoughts on the matter, that moral controversies are not serious ones – that they resemble discussions about our tastes, about what we like/dislike/desire/feel aversion to. In addition, it fails to account for two additional facts: that if we change our ethical convictions, we usually regard the previous ones as mistaken and false, and not simply as different, expressing our earlier attitudes; and that we cherish ethical doubts (which seem to be understandable only if we treat our ethical beliefs as *being able to be true*).

Third, antirealist moral naturalism undermines the normative character of moral rules: given their character (as it is understood within metaethical antirealism), it is by no means clear *why* we should obey them. Besides, it has relativistic implications: it follows from this view that moral rules are always relative to a concrete person or a group of persons (since if the meaning of ethical terms can be ultimately reduced to the mental states of a person, a group of persons, or even the whole mankind (species), then it cannot be said that a certain course of action is morally good *tout court* – it is always morally good for a given subject, more or less broadly understood).

The fourth argument for moral realism is that that one can make discoveries in the realm of morality. For instance, it was discovered only in Christian ethics that each human being has intrinsic dignity, or it was *not* discovered in antiquity that slavery is morally wrong. The very idea of discovering something in the realm of morality implies moral realism because one can only discover *moral truths*.

To these arguments I would like to add another, which appeals to evolutionary theory. This argument, as we shall see, is connected with the fourth argument, or can even be viewed as a variant of it.

3. AN EVOLUTIONARY ARGUMENT FOR NON-NATURALIST MORAL REALISM

Some philosophers have argued that evolutionary theory can be gainfully used to support antirealist moral naturalism (since the failure of social Darwinism, no attempts are nowadays made to appeal to evolutionary theory with a view to building normative theory on the basis of the 'laws of evolution', and thereby to argue for realist moral naturalism). Their argument proceeds in two steps. The first is the assumption that human beings have become endowed by natural selection with a disposition to act morally, and that thereby one can provide a plausible evolutionary genealogy of all of our moral dispositions. The second is the claim that by demonstrating an evolutionary genealogy of a disposition to take a moral act *P*, one thereby provides an argument for an antirealist character of a moral rule prescribing *P* – or, more precisely, one debunks this rule, that is, shows that we are not justified in endorsing it (should one defend a stronger claim – that by showing a defective origin of a belief one demonstrates its falsity – one would commit the so-called genetic fallacy). The second step can be justified in two different, though complementary, ways.

First, acting in accordance with rule *P* proves to be – besides whatever it may be beyond that – a means for achieving evolutionary success; it is therefore debunked as subservient to an evolutionary goal of transmitting one's genes to further generations, as a product of biological evolution designed to fulfil a specific function – that of most effectively spreading our genes. In other words, knowledge of the causes which lead us to formulate and accept moral rules strips those rules of their mysterious character: they are not a product of a 'truth-oriented' process; they prove to be simply 'correlates' of our evolved dispositions. It is therefore an illusion to believe that morality exists 'out there', independent of our dispositions, and discoverable by reason. This kind of reasoning is accepted, for instance, by Richard Joyce:

> Our moral beliefs are products of a process that is entirely independent of their truth, which forces the recognition that we have no grounds one way or other for maintaining these beliefs … I contend that on no epistemological theory worth its salt should the justificatory status of a belief remain unaffected by the discovery of an empirically supported theory that provides a compelling explanation of why we have that belief while nowhere presupposing its truth. (Joyce 2006: 211, 219)

Second, since each moral rule prescribing a course of action *P* is a 'correlate' of a biological disposition to do *P*, and the disposition could have been different if evolution took a different course (which is not an unrealistic assumption given that the course of evolution was determined to a large measure by chance events), moral rules should be interpreted in relativistic terms. Moral relativism, in turn, is strictly connected with moral antirealism. It is worth noting that although Darwin was not particularly interested in metaethical issues, one of his statements suggests that he might countenance at least the first part of this argument (concerning the relativistic implications of the evolutionary account of the origins of our moral propensities): he wrote that 'if bees had our mental faculties, they would have a sense of right and wrong but its content would be different' (Darwin 1871: 67). It is not by accident that Darwin writes 'different' rather than 'wrong': in this fragment he appears to imply that moral rules are not absolute but are connected with the circumstances in which human beings evolved.

The argument presented above leads its adherents to some version of moral antirealism. For instance, Michael Ruse (1995, 2006) and Richard Joyce (2000, 2006) assumed moral fictionalism. To quote Ruse:

> We see that morality has no philosophically objective foundation. It is just an illusion, fobbed off on us to promote biological 'altruism'. (Ruse 1995: 234)

> Substantive morality is a kind of illusion, put in place by our genes, in order to make us good social cooperators. I would add that the reason why the illusion is such a successful adaptation is that not only do we believe in substantive morality, but we also believe that substantive morality does have an objective foundation … I am arguing that the epistemological foundation of evolutionary ethics is a kind of moral non-realism, but that it is an

important part of evolutionary ethics that we think it is a kind of moral realism. (Ruse 2006: 21, 22)

Let me now move on to a critique of the evolutionary argument for metaethical antirealism. The argument is intended to refer to all moral systems, so it could be plausible as a general account of a metaethical status of *all moral statements* only if all moral systems could be demonstrated to be rooted in our evolved dispositions. But such a demonstration is not feasible for the simple reason that there are incompatible moral systems. Thus, this argument cannot be effective with regard to those moral systems which set requirements that do not have counterparts in our evolved dispositions, for instance, to such exacting moral systems as Christian ethics or Buddhist ethics. Christian ethics, for instance, prescribes such 'antievolutionary' duties as: practising universal love (*agape*), including love of one's enemies; non-violent resistance to evil; practising humility and unconditional forgiveness (and thereby opposing our reactive impulses); performing (heroic) acts in support of others even at the high cost of one's own life (though such acts are regarded in Christian ethics as supererogatory, not as obligatory); abstaining from morally judging other people; not attaching oneself to earthly goods; having pure thoughts and intentions; abandoning feelings of pride and moral self-contentment; attaining self-forgetfulness in the practice of goodness. Furthermore, it declares moral equality of all human beings irrespective of their race, nationality or sex. These rules could not be interpreted, even by the greatest feats of imagination, as serving the evolutionary goals of biological survival and reproduction. The same can be said about many other moral rules (absent in Christian ethics), for example those concerning our obligations to future generations, or proclaiming the moral irrelevance of sexual preference. They can be most plausibly interpreted as a result of autonomous moral reasoning liberated from the constraints of our evolved dispositions. The evolutionary argument for metaethical antirealism may therefore be plausible only with regard to moral systems which set requirements having counterparts in our evolved dispositions. If we assume this argument, it will turn out that evolutionary ethics (that is, ethics expressive of our innate moral dispositions, shaped by natural selection) is self-defeating: the very fact that it has an evolutionary genealogy – that we can explain how it came into being, and that this explanation implies that the goals of moral rules are very down to earth – undermines this ethics, which is therefore problematic in the sense that, given its origins, there seems to be no deeper reason why one should follow it. If the scope of this argument is circumscribed in this way, I find it convincing: moral rules that are part of evolutionary ethics are indeed debunked by their origins. But this cannot be the final word of the evolutionist on morality, since his debunking argument leaves genuine ethics intact. One can say even more: if one assumes that this debunking argument is valid (with regard to evolutionary ethics), then one must agree that it also provides *a contrario* a justification of genuine ethics (since its status cannot be reduced to that of the means to reproductive success), and thereby of moral non-naturalism (because genuine ethics is so distant from evolutionary ethics that it cannot be explained away as a projection of our natural propensities – as an illusion). Thus, Edward O. Wilson was only partly right when he wrote that 'human behaviour – like the deepest capacities for emotional response which drive and guide it – is the circuitous technique by which human genetic material has been and will be kept intact. Morality has no other demonstrable ultimate function' (Wilson 1978: 167); his view is correct with respect to evolutionary ethics, but is assuredly mistaken with respect to genuine ethics.

Some additional comments seem to be in order.

First, one may object that my evolutionary argumentation in favour of moral non-naturalism also undermines those rules of genuine ethics which it shares with evolutionary ethics, for instance, rules prohibiting theft, murder or deception. This objection would be apt only if these rules assumed the same form within both kinds of ethics, which is not the case. For instance, in its primitive form, the rule prohibiting murder makes a sharp distinction between the murder of a member of one's own group and that of members of another group: while the former is strongly condemned, the latter may be tolerated or even prescribed. Furthermore, even if the required action took the same form within evolutionary ethics and genuine ethics in its external aspect, the internal aspect is essentially different: genuine ethics puts stress on the moral purity of intentions, while evolutionary ethics is much less strict, if not indifferent, to intentions. As Francisco Ayala aptly remarked: 'the isomorphism between the behaviours promoted by natural selection and those sanctioned by moral norms exists only with respect to the consequences of the behaviours; the underlying causations are completely disparate' (Ayala 2010: 316). One should add that the 'common part' for evolutionary ethics and genuine ethics (corresponding to 'the rules of first layer', of which I wrote in the previous chapter) must exist because an ethical system which would be totally indifferent to biological survival and reproduction, and thereby did not treat them as values, would be self-defeating: populations accepting it would rapidly become extinct. The difference between these systems lies in the fact that genuine ethics, unlike evolutionary ethics, does not consider biological survival and reproduction to be the highest values, is more concerned with the purity of motivations and gives the common rules a more sophisticated (ethically purer) form.

Second, it is worth pointing to a somewhat paradoxical conclusion that seems to be implied by my evolutionary argument for moral non-naturalism. The evolutionarily optimistic picture of human nature, that is, one assuming that we have inbuilt propensities for genuinely moral actions, would be more dangerous for a non-naturalistic worldview, as it would deprive morality of its sublime, mysterious, 'otherworldly' character. The claim that human nature is flawed – evil or (doubly) ambivalent – better harmonizes with the belief in the (non-naturalistically) realist character of moral rules; what is more, it constitutes a strong argument for such a character of these rules.

Third, the evolutionary debunking of evolutionary ethics does not imply that evolutionary ethics could not have been a starting point for the development of genuine ethics. Reflection on evolutionary ethics and its limitations – made possible by human eminent intellectual capacities (to anticipate the future, to abstract thinking, to make free choices) – may have triggered a process which led to the 'purification' of the rules of evolutionary ethics and to further moral discoveries.

In the remainder of this chapter I shall develop the second step of my evolutionary argument for *ius*-naturalism (the first step, recall, was the evolutionary argumentation for moral non-naturalism). This second step in fact has two variants, as I shall propose two essentially different metaethical arguments for *ius*-naturalism.

4. THE FIRST METAETHICAL ARGUMENT FOR *IUS*-NATURALISM

This first metaethical argument (which could also be called 'an argument from the respect for law') is based on one metaethical premise, viz., that there is at least one true moral rule, viz. that 'laws, even bad laws, have a claim to our respect' (Fuller 1958: 630). This rule can be equivalently (or almost equivalently) stated in the following ways: 'laws, even bad laws, aspire to have a normative character'; 'there is a *prima facie* duty to obey legal rules'; 'there is a *prima facie* obligation of fidelity to law'; 'legal rules provide *prima facie* reasons for action'. The second premise of this argument states that any plausible conception of law ought to justify this moral rule; in other words, the definition of law 'must make meaningful the obligation of fidelity to law' (Fuller 1958: 635). The third premise is that the legal-positivistic account of law does not provide such a justification. The conclusion is therefore that legal positivism is not a plausible conception of law. The crucial, and most controversial, part of this argument is its third premise. Prior to examining it, however, I shall make some more general remarks on the problem of legal normativity (that is, on the first premise).

The problem of the normativity of legal rules boils down to the question of what features of a legal system justify the claim that legal rules provide reasons for action, and that thereby they give rise to 'Ought'. Clearly, the very fact that compliance with legal rules is enforced by the state by means of a system of sanctions does not provide a sufficient explanation of the normativity of law. If any system of rules enforced by sanctions could count as creating 'Ought', then even purely criminal organizations, unaccepted by citizens but exerting power over them, might be regarded as generating a system of rules endowed with 'Ought'. This is counterintuitive: for rules to be genuine *rules*, that is, to be endowed with 'Ought', they must be embedded not in – or not only in – the citizens' fear of sanctions for violating these rules; they must also give rise to their conviction that it is (at least *prima facie*) *right* to comply with these rules. Furthermore, I assume (as already mentioned) that the normativity of legal rules is strictly (conceptually) connected to the obligation to obey the law/the obligation of fidelity to law/the obligation to respect the law. This assumption is shared by most (but not all) legal positivists. For instance, that it was accepted by Herbert L.A. Hart can be inferred from his analysis of the decision to disobey the Nazi law, which he treated as a true moral dilemma 'in which the ideal of fidelity to law had to be sacrificed in favour of more fundamental goals' (Fuller 1958: 633). But this assumption was not accepted, for instance, by Joseph Raz (whose views I shall discuss later in this section).

How, then, can the normativity of legal rules be justified? There are two main approaches to this problem: the legal-positivistic and the *ius*-naturalistic. The first approach implies that the normativity of legal rules is to be strongly distinguished from the normativity of moral rules; 'legal Ought' is therefore essentially different from 'moral Ought'. The second approach implies that 'legal Ought' has a moral aspect, and therefore can be dubbed 'legal–moral Ought'. It is worth discussing these two approaches in somewhat greater detail.

According to the adherents of legal positivism, law is a system of rules created in a way determined by a specific social rule which Hart called 'a rule of recognition'. This rule determines the conditions of legal normativity, that is, it specifies what conditions must be satisfied for a legal rule to be created, modified, or annulled, or more generally for a rule to acquire a normative aspect of 'legal Ought'. On this view, law is therefore ultimately embedded in a social rule which is a special kind of social fact, viz. 'a form of judicial customary rule existing only if it is accepted and practiced in the law-identifying and law-applying operations of the courts' (Hart 1994: 256). This is the so-called Social Thesis of legal positivism; this thesis implies the so-called Separation Thesis, which says that there is no definitional connection between law and morality and that thereby it may be the case, if the rule of recognition does not count consistency with morality among the conditions of normativity of legal norms, that even immoral law is still law (cf., for example, Grabowski 2013). But given the Social Thesis of legal positivism, one may argue that legal positivism reduces 'legal Ought' to 'Is', that is, to a social fact, thus violating Hume's ban, and that thereby it does not provide an adequate explanation of the fact that legal rules provide reasons for action. In response to this criticism, a legal positivist may adopt four different strategies.

First, he may argue that the social fact in which 'legal Ought' is grounded is *a rule*, so that the justification of the normativity of legal rules is based on 'Ought' rather than on 'Is'. This argument, however, is not viable since the rule of recognition is conceived by legal positivists in factual terms – as a certain kind of social practice, viz. the practice of judges which consists in accepting and applying in their activities the law-identifying criteria.

Second, some legal philosophers (cf., for example, Postema 1982) have argued that the rule of recognition is a special kind of fact, namely, a social convention (in a game-theoretic sense), which by its very nature is normative and thereby can 'generate' legal normativity. The feature of the convention which is important in the context of the discussion about the sources of legal normativity is that it is a Nash equilibrium and thereby is self-enforcing – that is, no one has an interest in violating a convention if everyone follows it. In other words, the normativity of conventions directly stems from the requirements of instrumental rationality. Now, if the rule of recognition were a social convention in the game-theoretic sense, one could say that normativity (in the sense of instrumental rationality) is, so to speak, built into it, and is subsequently 'transmitted' from it to lower order (primary) legal rules. It is by no means clear, however, that the rule of recognition is a social convention (in the game-theoretic sense). One can raise at least two arguments against this interpretation of the rule of recognition: (1) it is not very plausible to maintain that judges follow the rule of recognition just because it is generally practised; it seems they have other (or additional but more important) reasons to follow it, for example, their reason for regarding legislation as a source of law may be that it is a democratic and economically efficient method of lawmaking (cf. Green 1999: 39–40); (2) it can hardly be argued that for each rule of recognition one can imagine an alternative rule that enables achieving the same purpose (and therefore that the rule of recognition is arbitrary in the relevant sense); thus, it is hard to maintain that the choice of a particular variant of a rule of recognition is of no or little importance.

Third, one may reject or weaken the Social Thesis of legal positivism. This step was taken by Hans Kelsen (1967), whose so-called 'pure theory of law' is sometimes dubbed 'critical legal positivism' (though one may justifiably ask whether a theory of law that rejects the Social Thesis can still be regarded as a version – even if critical – of legal positivism). Kelsen treated the fact that the law's requirements are imposed by sanctions as its essential feature. In his view, thus understood, law is a unique entity (quite separate from morality, as well as from natural and social facts) which belongs to a nonfactual sphere of *Sollen* ('Ought'). Kelsen therefore posited the existence of a separate sphere of *Sollen* (as opposed to the sphere of *Sein*), where he 'located' legal norms. This view encounters various difficulties (for example, it is not clear whether the distinction between *Sollen* and *Sein* is ontological or only epistemological, or to which sphere moral norms belong) which need not be discussed here in detail. The point that is important in this context is how Kelsen introduced 'legal Ought', that is, legal normativity. Now, Kelsen claimed that *the normativity of law is presupposed by each legal system.* More precisely, in Kelsen's view, each and every effectively functioning legal system presupposes the Basic Norm – a kind of norm that 'confers' normativity on the entire legal system (from constitution through statutes to judicial decisions) and thereby gives rise to the sphere of 'legal *Sollen*'. Kelsen justified this claim by means of transcendental argumentation. He started from the assumption that legal rules possess a normative aspect, that is, that they provide reasons for action, and then posed the question as to what must be presupposed for this normative aspect to be conceivable. His answer was that what must be presupposed is the Basic Norm. The notion of the Basic Norm as the source of normativity of all the other legal norms enabled Kelsen to avoid the task (undertaken, in fact, by 'noncritical' legal positivists) of deriving 'legal Ought' from 'Is'.

Fourth, I have assumed that the normativity of legal rules is strictly (conceptually) connected to the obligation to obey the law, or the obligation of fidelity to law/the obligation to respect the law. But, as was already mentioned, such equivalence was explicitly rejected by Joseph Raz, who claimed that there is no general, even *prima facie*, obligation to obey the law (just because it is the law); the obligation may arise only if one respects the law, and that respect itself is not a morally required attitude, but only a permissible one: one may just as well be morally indifferent to the law (cf. Raz 1979: 233, 250). Law, in Raz's view, is an authoritative power: it formulates second-order, exclusionary reasons for action, that is, reasons to refrain from acting (in the context of actions regulated by law) on other than legal reasons. But the authority of law, demanding 'not only the obedience, but the allegiance of its subjects' (Raz 1979: 236), is conditional – yet to be justified (otherwise it would, as if automatically, give rise to the duty of obedience/respect). The essential feature of law is therefore not legitimate (moral–political) authority as such, but a claim to such authority, which may not be justified. As Raz put it: 'The law claims that its rules and rulings are authoritative. To establish an obligation (in the strong sense) to obey the law, as commonly understood, is to establish that its claim is justified, that the law indeed has the legitimate authority it claims to have' (Raz 1979: 237). Accordingly, Raz's strategy seems to consist in depriving the normativity of law of almost any normative content: the normativity arises only when it is demonstrated that the claim to (moral–political) authority is justified.

None of these four strategies seems satisfactory. The first omits the fact that the rule of recognition is a social fact (even if a complex one, embracing a set of normative convictions of judges), and thereby cannot justify the normative character of the law. The second makes a controversial assumption that the rule of recognition is a social convention. The question of whether the rule of recognition is a social convention, however, is still an open one. For instance, Andrei Marmor (2009) argues that the rule of recognition can be regarded as a convention, giving rise to a specifically 'legal Ought', on condition that that convention is conceived of as *constitutive* (rather than, as within game theory, as coordinative) – that is, as *constituting the very phenomenon of law*. The third introduces *ad hoc* the Basic Norm, whose ontological status is notoriously unclear, and more importantly allows one to speak only about 'relative', 'hypothetical', 'conditional' normativity, as Kelsen himself admits in his article *Die philosophischen Grundlagen der Naturrechtslehre und des Rechtpositivismus*. The fourth seems to be rather untypical for legal positivism: it becomes hard to distinguish it from a milder version of *ius*-naturalism (to be defended in later in this chapter) which makes a distinction between *lex* and *legis corruptio* (on Raz's theory, a law which raises an unjustified claim to authority/legitimacy might be called precisely *legis corruptio* – a flawed, corrupted law). If one wanted to avoid treating Raz as crypto *ius*-naturalist, one could argue that the very claim to authority is tantamount to the existence of the *prima facie* duty to obey the law, and therefore needs to be justified. But, of course, this is inconsistent with Raz's explicit statements about the separation between the claim to authority and the obligation to obey the law, and – furthermore – does not resolve the problem of the sources of the normativity of law. Accordingly, it seems that legal positivism does not tackle effectively the problem of the sources of legal normativity, or, more precisely, cannot justify the *prima facie* moral obligation to obey the law. The dilemma of the legal positivist was elegantly captured by Lon L. Fuller and Joel Feinberg. According to Fuller, law, as it is conceived by legal positivists, is an 'amoral datum', which is supposed to have 'a peculiar quality of creating a moral duty to obey it'; however, in Fuller's (apt) opinion, if law is understood in this way, then it cannot give rise to such a duty:

> I do not think it is unfair to the positivistic philosophy to say that it never gives any coherent meaning to the moral obligation of fidelity to law. This obligation seems to be conceived as *sui generis*, wholly unrelated to any of the ordinary, extralegal ends of human life. The fundamental postulate of positivism – that law must be strictly severed from morality – seems to deny the possibility of any bridge between the obligation to obey the law and other moral obligations. (Fuller 1958: 656)

As a result, Fuller wrote about 'the essential incapacity of the positivistic view to serve this ideal [of fidelity to law – WZ]' (Fuller 1958: 642). Feinberg wrote in similar vein:

> the two doctrines of validity [accepted by legal positivists – WZ] by pedigree and respect for law as such yield in combination an unstable conception of law as 'an amoral datum' [Lon L. Fuller's term – WZ] that has a kind of magical capacity to generate moral obligations. One easy way out for the positivist, and I think the only way, is to abandon the second doctrine, and admit that there is no moral duty whatever to obey law simply because it is valid law. (Feinberg 1994: 159)

Is there any other way of defending legal positivism than the (radical) one proposed by Feinberg? One might argue that what justifies the rule of recognition is the kind of political system in which laws are enacted, viz. the democratic system. The problem is that the austere doctrine of legal positivism is insensitive to the kind of power which enacts law. It is true that legal positivism is much more plausible in the context of democratic systems than, say, in the context of authoritarian or dictatorial regimes acting against the will of their subjects. But legal positivism does not contain any resources which would enable one to justify a choice of a political system.

In summary, if one assumes that the notion of legal normativity is conceptually linked to the notion of an obligation to obey the law, it turns out that the positivistic account of normativity does not respect this assumption: it is not plausible to maintain that we have an obligation to obey the law just because it is the law if law's normativity is understood in a legal-positivistic manner, viz. as allowing the situation in which immoral rules are valid. Legal positivism may be a plausible description of only those parts of a legal system which do not have a moral dimension. In point of fact, even some legal positivists, such as the Polish legal theorist Tomasz Gizbert-Studnicki, concede that legal positivism 'cannot satisfactorily resolve … the problem of the normativity of law' (Gizbert-Studnicki 2017: 35), and thereby can only be regarded as a 'minimum theory'. They do not treat it, however, as a sufficient reason for searching for a 'full-blooded' theory of law. For instance, Gizbert-Studnicki claims that the solution of the problem of normativity (that is, the account of the factors that make legal rules provide genuine reasons for action) should be sought in political philosophy. But this solution seems to posit an artificial boundary between legal philosophy, political philosophy and morality. Why not search for a more open-ended theory of law, which would transcend those boundaries?

The problem of the normativity of law, and consequently of the justification of the *prima facie* duty to obey the law, is effectively tackled by *ius*-naturalism. According to the classical theories of natural law, law is a system of *right* rules, that is, rules concordant with morality. This basic claim common to all classical natural law theories implies that among the necessary conditions of legal normativity (that is, conditions that render any putative norm legally valid) there is the requirement of concordance with morality. In consequence: *lex iniusta non est lex* – unjust law is not law. Thus, the source of normativity of legal norms lies in morality: legal 'Ought' is *partly* reduced to moral 'Ought'. It is worth noting that one can imagine an *extreme* version of natural law theories according to which concordance with morality is a necessary *and sufficient* condition of the normativity of a legal rule; on this version legal 'ought' is *entirely* reduced to moral 'ought'. But such a version was not supported by any serious representative of *ius*-naturalism. Hart wrote that 'it could not follow from the mere fact that a rule violated standards of morality that it was not a rule of law; and, conversely, it could not follow from the mere fact that a rule was morally desirable that it was a rule of law' (Hart 1958: 599). He characterized legal positivism in this passage, but the second part of it is also accepted by *ius*-naturalists. According to the dominant (and, in fact the only plausible) version of *ius*-naturalism, the source of normativity of (human-made) legal norms lies in morality, but one cannot speak about legal rules if some additional conditions are not fulfilled, that is, if legal rules have not been adopted in a proper way determined by some 'rule of recognition'. For instance, Thomas Aquinas wrote in *Summa Theologiae* (I-II, q. 90, a. 4) that *Lex est quaedam rationis ordinatio ad bonum commune, ab eo qui curam communitatis habet, promulgata*; he therefore explicitly stated that the law must be promulgated. As can be easily seen, the theories of natural law imply that the source of the normativity of legal rules is more variegated than the source of the normativity of moral rules: while moral rules acquire their normative character only by virtue of their satisfying certain criteria of moral acceptability (determined by a given moral theory, for example, Kantianism or utilitarianism), legal rules become normative if and only if they satisfy the criteria of moral acceptability *and* have been properly enacted, that is, in accordance with some social rule which provides conditions for creating legal rules (though perhaps it would be more apt to say that, on the *ius*-naturalistic theories, legal rules are *rules*, that is, provide reasons for action – and thereby they are normative – because they are concordant with moral rules, and are *legal* rather than moral, because they satisfy the conditions of 'legality' provided by some rule of recognition). Since natural law theories embed 'legal Ought' in moral 'Ought', the former has in fact a moral aspect too; hence, on the ground of the *ius*-naturalistic theories of law, 'legal Ought' is in fact 'legal–moral Ought'.

Some additional clarifications regarding *ius*-naturalism seem to be necessary.

First, the phrase *lex iniusta non est lex* can be given different senses. It may mean, as the literal reading suggests, that the unjust law is not a law at all; this reading seems to have been assumed by St Augustine, who wrote in *De libero arbitrio* (I, 5, 11) that *nam mihi lex esse non videtur, quae iusta non fuerit*. But it must be admitted that St Augustine does not develop this insight, so it is not entirely justifiable to assign to him a specific version of *ius*-naturalism. Or this phrase may mean it is not a law in the full sense, but a corruption of law, a defective law: *lex iniusta non est lex sed legis corruptio* (*Summa Theologiae* I-II, q. 95. a. 2c). On the first (let me call it 'Augustinian') reading, morality is directly connected to the legal validity of a norm, and on the latter (Thomist) reading, it is connected to its nondefectiveness. The difference between these two readings might seem to be purely verbal: one might claim that the only interesting consequence of the discrepancy between a legal rule and morality seems to be that the legal rule does not give rise to a duty of obedience, and whether we say that it is because of the law's invalidity or defectiveness is of no importance. But this does not seem to be the case.

The adoption of the first reading would expose a *ius*-naturalist to the objection that he refuses to give the name 'law' to systems of rules which are effective and regarded by law as its subjects. *Ius*-naturalism on the second reading (which does not claim that immoral law is not a law, but, rather, *legis corruptio*) avoids this objection: its adherents may respond to it by saying that the legal systems are legal systems, but corrupted/perverted ones, that is, not legal systems in the full sense; they can therefore speak about past immoral legal systems as (corrupted) legal systems.

Second, the theories of natural law, in contradistinction to legal positivism, have no difficulty with finding sources of legal normativity: the source is 'moral Ought'. Their success in this regard, however, is achieved as a result of introducing a controversial concept of 'natural law'. It is banal to say that this concept was given various meanings over history. The most general line of division is between the theories whose central notion is that of 'natural law' and those whose central notion is that of 'natural rights' (cf. Strauss 1965; Finnis 1980). The former, which are historically older, have the following features: they are focused on human duties, not on human rights – 'if they paid any attention at all to the rights of man, they conceived of them as essentially derivative from his duties' (Strauss 1965: 182); they assume a teleological worldview, that is, the existence of natural *teloi* – goals which each natural entity, including the human being, is supposed to attain if it is to attain perfection; accordingly, they expect much of the law, that is, they assign to it an important role in realizing *summum bonum* of human beings, or human excellence. They are therefore perfectionist and conservative. A particularly important variant of these theories is the theological strand, the most famous of which is St Thomas Aquinas' assumption that legal 'ought' can be ultimately reduced to – or is identical with – Divine 'is', God himself, because – in his view – in God, 'ought' becomes indiscernible from 'is'. The latter theories are focused on human rights, need not assume a teleological worldview and usually treat natural rights as 'self-evident'; they consider an individual to have priority over a society; they are more focused on combating *malum* than realizing *summum bonum*. They are therefore antiperfectionist, or liberal; the role of the state is not so much to assure human excellence (which is a controversial notion on the basis of these theories), but simply of 'commodious living' (Strauss 1965: 182). These theories are easier to reconcile with the contemporary scientific worldview which dispenses with the teleological elements. But the differences between various theories of natural law should not be overestimated. They are not essential, that is, they concern less the content of rules of natural law than the general philosophical framework in which they are placed. There seems to be a large consensus among people who have devoted their intellectual activity to the analysis of moral issues as to what moral rules are the right ones. Essentially, moral sages – the Stoic, the Christian, the Buddhist, or others – are, basically, in agreement with each other. Related to the problem of variability of natural law is another problem of *ius*-naturalism, viz. what morality should serve as a basis for assessing the validity of legal rules: conventional morality accepted in a given time in a given society (whose legal system is subject to moral evaluation), or genuine (enlightened, critical) morality. There is no doubt that it should be the latter. This may lead to a somewhat paradoxical situation (which must be boldly accepted by a *ius*-naturalist) that a given law is (or was) regarded as valid and noncorrupt by its subjects (who accept the law as consistent with their morality), but would be considered as corrupt by a theorist professing genuine morality.

Third, the critics of *ius*-naturalism often argue that the conception of legal validity implied by this tradition undermines legal certainty and thereby weakens public trust in legal institutions; they treat this objection to natural law as one of the arguments for legal positivism. However, this argument may be correct only with regard to one, rather extreme, conception of natural law, according to which: (1) natural law is a system of *numerous* and *specific* moral rules 'duplicating' a legal system; (2) the inconsistency of a legal rule with a corresponding moral rule *ipso facto* discharges subjects from the duty to obey the law. One can, however, defend conceptions of natural law which are resistant to the objection of undermining legal certainty and diminishing public trust in legal institutions; furthermore, these conceptions, even if they did undermine legal certainty to a greater degree than legal positivism, would be likely to increase public trust in legal institutions as compared with legal positivism. Two such conceptions are worth discussing. The first assumes that (1) natural law exists but is, basically, unknowable; (2) and its role for assessing legal rules does not consist in assessing their validity or the degree of their corruption but in generating in society a critical stance towards legal rules, or, in other words, in preventing legal positivism (according to which a legal rule is valid if it was adopted in accordance with the rule of recognition) from transforming into ethical positivism (according to which a legal rule which is valid is *ipso facto* an ethical rule). The conception, however, is rather odd. It could be used to justify legal positivism, for if we assume that moral realism is true but it is impossible to decide which of the proposed moral rules is the right one, then the task of the legislator would be in fact to make an arbitrary choice between them. Since, *ex hypothesi*, there is no independent criterion of choosing rules, this view would, for all practical purposes, be legal positivism (rather than something intermediate between *ius*-naturalism and legal positivism). The second conception, which is more plausible, assumes that (1) natural law does not embrace numerous and specific moral rules but only *few*, *fundamental* and *general* ones; (2) and the inconsistency of a legal rule with one of those principles does not *ipso facto* discharge the subjects from the duty to obey the law, since the object of assessment in terms of validity is the legal system as a whole. In other words, if a legal system satisfied, in general, the demands of morality (justice), then a particular immoral legal rule (which, as regards its immorality, is therefore an exception) should be obeyed. Element (1) of this view is taken from Gustave Radbruch's theory of natural law which implies that legal rules are not valid if they violate only the most basic (that is, especially important) moral norms (that is, not just any moral norms): *lex iniustissima* (not *iniusta*) *non est lex*. Element (2) can be ascribed to Thomas Aquinas (*Summa Theologiae*, q. 96), who believed that unjust law (that is, law which, according to his definition, is adopted not for the common good but for the good or vainglory of the ruler; or law which was adopted by the ruler overstepping the boundaries of his competence; or law which serves the common good but unjustly and disproportionately distributes burdens among members of a community) is *legis corruptio* – an act of violence which does not bind conscience *unless* obedience to law is necessary for the avoidance of moral scandal and social unrest (*nisi forte propter vitandum scandalum vel turbationem*). Finally, one should repeat here the observation previously made that large areas of law are morally indifferent/neutral, and thus unregulated by natural law. Thus, the fear that *ius*-naturalism may undermine legal certainty is also, for that reason, unjustified: large areas of law will correspond to the legal-positivistic understanding of law, that is, the validity of many legal rules will be assessed by reference to their 'pedigree', not to their content.

5. THE SECOND METAETHICAL ARGUMENT FOR *IUS*-NATURALISM

The second metaethical argument for *ius*-naturalism can be presented, in its general form, in this way. It is uncontroversial to say that if metaethical realism is false, one cannot endorse the *ius*-naturalistic approach to the problem of the sources of legal normativity, since the theories of natural law assume the existence of 'moral Ought' and metaethical antirealism implies that 'moral Ought' is a fiction. But more interestingly (and controversially), if metaethical realism is true, one cannot endorse legal positivism, since legal positivism is logically incoherent with metaethical realism (the stronger version), or disharmonious with metaethical realism (the weaker version). I shall develop the two versions of this argument at greater length.

THE STRONGER VERSION

Premises

1. *Ius*-naturalism implies metaethical realism.
2. Legal positivism implies metaethical antirealism.
3. Metaethical realism is true (that is, is a correct metaethical view).

Conclusion 1: Legal positivism is false.

Additional premise: Either *ius*-naturalism or legal positivism is true.

Conclusion 2: *Ius*-naturalism is true.

This argument is formally valid but materially invalid, or at least highly controversial as far as its premise 2 is concerned, because many (or most) legal positivists reject the claim that legal positivism implies metaethical antirealism. But this argument is effective with regard to those (rare) varieties of legal positivism which are based on metaethical antirealism. Arguably, Hans Kelsen, one of the greatest legal positivists, accepted such a variety of legal positivism, and thereby the stronger version of the argument (with premise 3 changed, of course, but with the essential premises 1 and 2). Kelsen's argument in favour of legal positivism can be reconstructed as follows:

1. *Ius*-naturalism implies metaethical realism.
2. Legal positivism implies metaethical antirealism.
3. Metaethical antirealism is true.

Conclusion 1: Ius-naturalism is false.

Additional premise: Either *ius*-naturalism or legal positivism is true.

Conclusion 2: Legal positivism is true.

One needs to justify the claim that Kelsen indeed accepted this argument. In his essay *Was ist Gerechtigkeit?* Kelsen wrote explicitly that not only the rankings of values but also values themselves are subjective; there are therefore no absolute, objective values, that is, values whose existence would not depend on our mental activity:

> Real judgments of value are subjective … When our conscience requires absolute justification of our behavior, i.e., postulates absolute values, it turns out that our reason is not in a position to satisfy this requirement … Absolute justice is an irrational ideal. (*Echte Werturteile subjekiver sind … Wenn unser Gewissen absolute Rechtertigung unseres Verhalten fordert, d.h. aber absolute Werte postuliert, so ist unsere Vernunft nich imstande, diese Forderung zu erfüllen … Absolute Gerechtigkeit ist ein irrationales Ideal.*) (Kelsen 2003: 11, 26, 49)

In this passage he openly declares his axiological subjectivism and (the consequent) relativism. It can be therefore safely assumed that Kelsen believed in metaethical antirealism, that is, premise 3. Incidentally, he also believed that from his 'relativistic philosophy of justice' (*relativistische Gerechtigkeitsphilosophie*) one can deduce the principle of tolerance (cf. Kelsen 2003: 49), but this deduction is somewhat mysterious and introduces an element of 'absolutism' to his theory in a rather *ad hoc* fashion; I omit this element of his theory, as it is not important in the context of my analysis. Apart from premise 3, he also explicitly assumed premises 1 and 2; in his article *Die philosophischen Grundlagen der Naturrechtslehre und des Rechtpositivismus*, he asserted that 'positivism and (epistemological) relativism are connected with each other in such a way as *ius*-naturalism with (metaphysical) absolutism … Law of nature, by virtue of its provenance, comes from absolute values and absolute validity' (Kelsen 2017: 25–6). He emphasized that the positivistic conception of the legal system excludes the recognition of the existence of a higher legal order, the order of the law of nature (cf. Kelsen 2017: 51). Such a claim only makes sense if one assumes that the deeper philosophical underpinnings of legal positivism and *ius*-naturalism are contradictory: the former, in Kelsen's view, implies metaethical antirealism and naturalistic monism, and the latter metaethical realism and metaphysical dualism.

One should stress, however, a certain lack of clarity in Kelsen's views. In the above quoted passage he emphasized that his relativism was of 'epistemological' nature, that is, that his claim was not that there are no absolute values but that we cannot know if they exist. A similar declaration can be found in his essay *Was ist Gerechtigkeit?*:

> In fact I do not know and cannot say what justice is, absolute justice, this beautiful dream of men. I must satisfy myself with relative justice, and can only say what justice is for me. (*Und in der Tat, ich weiss nicht und kann nicht sagen, was Gerechtigkeit ist, die absolute Gerechtigkeit, dieser schöne Traum der Menschheit. Ich muss mich mit einer relative Gerechtigkeit begnügen und kann nur sagen, was Gerechtigkeit für mich ist.*) (Kelsen 2003: 52)

Analogously, he asserted that the rejection of metaphysical dualism has an epistemological, noncategorical character: this rejection is 'a conscious self-limitation of the human spirit, which knows that the world of experience is surrounded with mysteries, which cannot be probed by reason' (Kelsen 2017: 93). These passages are in tension with his aforementioned unequivocal statements about the subjective and relative character of values, about absolute values being 'an irrational ideal'. Furthermore, Kelsen's declaration of epistemological modesty, of his respect for mystery of human existence, is somewhat at odds with his rather simplistic psychological analyses of those who accept legal positivism and those who accept *ius*-naturalism; the former are supposed to be objective, disinterested in their cognition, whereas the latter are supposed to be moved by wishful thinking (cf. Kelsen 2017: 96). But even if he were 'only' an epistemological relativist and subjectivist (or, equivalently, an agnostic about values), this would not change the core of his argument, which – if he were agnostic about values – would then take the following form:

Premises:

1. *Ius*-naturalism implies metaethical realism.
2. Legal positivism implies metaethical antirealism *or* (at least) agnosticism with respect to values (their existence and/or content).
3. Agnosticism (epistemological relativism) with respect to values is true.

Conclusion 1: Ius-naturalism is false.

Additional premise: Either *ius*-naturalism or legal positivism is true.

Conclusion 2: Legal positivism is true.

In summary, according to Kelsen, legal positivism can be accepted only if we assume that natural law (absolute values) does not exist, or it cannot be known whether it exists or not, or it is known to exist but its content cannot be known. If it exists and its content can be known, then legal positivism, which implies metaethical antirealism or agnosticism, proves to be logically incoherent (given the truthfulness of metaethical realism and the possibility of knowing values). But natural law does not exist, or it cannot be known whether it exists or not, or its content cannot be known. Therefore legal positivism is true. It may be noted in passing that a similar argument seems to have been made by Gustave Radbruch, who in his positivistic, 'prewar' period openly declared his agnosticism, and in his *ius*-naturalistic, postwar period rejected it, thereby making a strong link between the legal-philosophical and metaethical views.

Even though the above, stronger version of the metaethical argument (with premise 3 changed but the essential premises 1 and 2 preserved) was accepted by an eminent legal-positivist thinker of this stature, one cannot ascribe it to most positivists (Kelsen and, arguably, Radbruch would therefore be exceptions). Most legal positivists – for example, Herbert L.A. Hart (1994), Joseph Raz (1979) or Tomasz Gizbert-Studnicki (2017) – seem to believe that the theses of legal positivism can be formulated without reference to the problems of metaethics; they therefore explicitly reject the premise that legal positivism *implies* metaethical realism. For instance, Hart (who was arguably a metaethical antirealist) invoked the fact that the 'fathers' of legal positivism – John Austin and Jeremy Bentham – were metaethical realists: Austin believed in the existence of objective, divine law, consisting of the commands of God, which are known either directly, by God's revelation, or indirectly, by considerations regarding social utility; Bentham was a naturalist moral realist, claiming that moral statements are verifiable statements about social utility. The moral Hart draws is that one can be a legal positivist irrespective of one's metaethical views. The way in which most legal positivists connect legal-philosophical and metaethical views can be more precisely reconstructed as follows:

Premises:

1. *Ius*-naturalism implies metaethical realism.
2. Legal positivism is indifferent with regard to metaethical views.

Conclusion: Even if we agree that metaethical realism is a correct view it will have no implications whatsoever for the controversy between *ius*-naturalism and legal positivism.

Most legal positivists would therefore assert that the metaethical view can influence legal-philosophical views in only one way: if a legal theorist assumes metaethical antirealism, then *ius*-naturalism is not a possible option for him (because, obviously, *ius*-naturalism implies metaethical realism). They are indeed right to claim that legal positivism does not *imply* metaethical antirealism, and consequently that there is no logical inconsistency between legal positivism and metaethical realism. But they do not take into account the fact that even though legal positivism and metaethical realism are not mutually inconsistent, they nonetheless do not constitute a harmonious whole. The weaker version of the metaethical argument tries to explicate the sense in which these two views do not jibe well – do not harmonize – with each other.

THE WEAKER VERSION

Premises:

1. *Ius*-naturalism implies metaethical realism.
2. Legal positivism is indifferent with regard to metaethical views.
3. Metaethical realism is true.

4a. Each theory of legal normativity (validity) should avoid *doubling* the kinds of normativity, and thereby *introducing a crevice* in the realm of normativity; accordingly, if moral normativity does exist, then introducing an entirely disparate kind of normativity will amount to introducing a crevice in the realm of normativity.

4b. Moral normativity is stronger than (purely) legal normativity. If the former exists, then introducing the latter, that is, defining legal normativity without reference to moral normativity, would be idiosyncratic: it would in fact amount to discounting the existence of moral normativity, or even worse: implicitly, and mistakenly, treating it as nonexistent.

4c. If a legal theorist agrees that there exist moral truths and that the legislator ought to be guided by them while enacting law, then he cannot maintain that the violation of the requirement of being guided by moral truths is of no consequence for the question of the validity of law.

4d. Take two mutually contradictory views *A* and *B*. If *A* implies *C*, while *B* is indifferent to *C* (does not imply either *C* or non-*C*), then the truth of *C* is a *prima facie* reason to accept *A* rather than *B*.

Conclusion: Ius-naturalism is a more plausible – because more harmonious (given the premise of metaethical realism) – view than legal positivism.

I do not insist on the truthfulness of premise 4d – an axiom which seems plausible but would assuredly deserve a closer analysis. At any rate, if it were true, it would formally decide that, assuming metaethical realism, one ought to accept *ius*-naturalism. The argument could then be called a variant of the strong one. For my purposes, however, it is sufficient that *any* of the variants of premise 4 is true (they may also be jointly true, for they do not exclude each other).

How could a legal positivist criticize this argument?

First, he could contend that metaethical realism is not only noncontradictory with legal positivism (which is conceded by this argument), but in fact stays in harmony with it. Hart made this point in the following way:

> Let us now suppose that we accept the rejection of 'non-cognitive' theories of morality and this denial of the drastic distinction in type between statements of what is and what ought to be, and that moral judgments are as rationally defensible as any other kind of judgments. What would follow from this as to the nature of the connection between law as it is and law as it ought to be? Surely, from this alone, nothing. Laws, however morally iniquitous, would still (so far as this point is concerned) be laws. The only difference which the acceptance of this view of the nature of moral judgments would make would be that the moral iniquity of such laws would be something that could be demonstrated; it would surely follow merely from a statement of what the rule required to be done that the rule was morally wrong and so ought not to be law or conversely that it was morally desirable and ought to be law. But the demonstration of this would not show the rule not to be (or to be) law. Proof of the principles by which we evaluate or condemn laws are rationally discoverable, and not mere 'fiats of the will', leaves untouched the fact that there are laws which may have any degree of iniquity or stupidity and still be laws. And conversely there are rules that have every moral qualification to be laws and yet are not laws. (Hart 1958: 626)

The 'only difference' of which Hart writes, viz. that the iniquity could be demonstrated, is, contrary to what Hart seems to imply, a serious difference. It makes a full-fledged moral critique of law possible, and makes the very conflict between a legal and a moral rule something of primary importance – all the more so if we do not simply demonstrate once it has been enacted that a given legal rule is iniquitous, but know this fact beforehand (given that *ius*-naturalism, on its most plausible version, assumes that the rules of natural law are few and fundamental). If we assume an antirealist (noncognitivist) theory, it would not be clear why we ought to be concerned with this conflict. But if the conflict takes on a really serious character, as it does on metaethically realist grounds, then the very postulate of consistency between law and morality becomes a matter of primary importance, paving the way for the *ius*-naturalist position.

Second, a legal positivist might also say also that the argument *may be* compelling with regard only to such metaethically realist positions which are axiologically monistic or weakly pluralistic, but not with regard to those which are strongly pluralistic. Let me briefly present these varieties of metaethical realism. Axiological monism assumes that there is only one objective value (or, equivalently, one moral duty); all other values are reducible to it. Examples of such views are utilitarianism (the only value is social utility/happiness) or hedonism (the only value is pleasure). Axiological pluralism assumes that there are many *different*, that is, irreducible to each other, objective values. In its weakest variant it assume that values are *compatible*, that is, they do not come into conflict with each other (and thereby can always be realized at the same time). In its weak variant it assumes that values are *incompatible* but *commensurable*, that is, they come into conflict with each other but these conflicts can be rationally resolved because values can be hierarchically graded (the hierarchy of values, like values themselves, is objective). In its strong variant (defended, for example, by Isaiah Berlin), axiological pluralism assumes that values are *incompatible* and *incommensurable*. This is not the proper place to analyse in depth the tricky concept of incommensurability, but some quick remarks may be in order here. One can define it imprecisely as the claim that there does not exist an objective hierarchy of values, or that values cannot be compared to each other, or that there is not one correct answer to moral dilemmas. A more precise definition of incommensurability was provided by Joseph Raz: ‘A and B are incommensurable if it is neither true that one is better than the other nor true that they are of equal values’ (Raz 1988: 322). In Raz’s view, incommensurability differs from equality in that the former implies ‘that an option may be better than one of the two incommensurate options without being better than the other’ (Raz 1988: 325). Thus, ‘the test of incommensurability is failure of transitivity: two valuable options are incommensurate if (1) neither is better than the other, and (2) there is (or could be) another option which is better than one but is not better than the other’ (Raz 1988: 325). Raz emphasizes that the failure of transitivity is not a part of the definition of incommensurability, but rather its ‘mark’. It is worth noting that Raz’s account (his test of transitivity) seems to imply that the *full commensurability of values is incoherent*: at least some values must be commensurable in order to speak meaningfully about the incommensurability of other values. At any rate, (strong) value pluralists assume at least that *many* objective values are incompatible and incommensurable. Now, a legal positivist may claim that strong pluralism of values provides a reason for accepting legal positivism. In a situation of the conflict and incommensurability of values the legislator is not bound by natural law, even if it exists, since it says nothing about methods of solving the conflicts of values, and thereby has full discretion in resolving these conflicts (for instance, between liberty and equality, justice and social welfare, liberty and security, equality of opportunity and equality of outcome, equity and formal justice, freedom of access to information and privacy, freedom of movement and right of ownership, etc.). This view seems to have been defended by Herbert L.A. Hart, who wrote as follows (making reference to his conception of the minimum content of natural law, which I have described in Chapter 2):

> in asking what content a legal system must have we take this question to be worth asking only if we who consider it cherish the humble aim of survival in close proximity to our fellows. Natural-law theory, however, in all its protean guises, attempts to push the argument much farther and to assert that human beings are equally devoted to and united in their conception of aims (the pursuit of knowledge, justice to their fellow men) other than that of survival, and these dictate a further necessary content to a legal system (over and above my humble minimum) without which it would be pointless. Of course we must be careful not to exaggerate the differences among human beings, but it seems to me that above this minimum the purposes men have for living in society are too conflicting and varying to make possible much extension of the argument that some fuller overlap of legal rules and moral standards is 'necessary' in this sense.

But this conclusion is hard to accept. The legislator is still bound by *objective* values; he is not to make arbitrary decisions: he must always choose one or some of the conflicting objective values, or make some tradeoff between them. Furthermore, as was already mentioned, full incommensurability of values is an incoherent idea (some values must be compared in order to use the test of transitivity). Thus, it is implausible to maintain that strong pluralism justifies or leads to legal positivism. This does not mean, of course, that pluralism of values does not have interesting philosophical consequences. They do not concern, however, the controversy between legal positivism and *ius*-naturalism. Strong pluralism of values implies, for instance, that – as was emphasized especially by Isaiah Berlin – the very idea of perfection, which seems to imply that there is only one correct hierarchy of values, turns out to be incoherent. Accordingly, the ideas of a perfect society, of perfect social harmony, of a happy life, of a perfect life, of a perfect man (realizing all values/virtues), or of progress towards some ideal seem to be incoherent (cf. Polanowska-Sygulska 2008). One should not, however, understand this insight too radically: even assuming strong pluralism of values, one can reasonably speak about ethical progress (for example, from evolutionary ethics to genuine ethics), as it may consist in discovering new values, eliminating pseudovalues, and 'purifying' the already known values. Furthermore, Berlin also claimed (more controversially) that if strong pluralism of values is true, then the state is never justified in imposing a particular rank of values on its citizens. Strong pluralism of values therefore increases the importance of one specific value (or metavalue), viz. individual (negative) freedom, which, according to

Berlin, should be as broad as possible, because it enables citizens to make their own choices among conflicting values. It therefore implies condemnation of a government's illiberal actions. But some disagree with this view; for example, John Gray (2000) claims that strong pluralism of values subverts liberalism, because it implies that liberalism is only one of many *valuable* social/political life forms, which cannot be compared to each other – to claim that liberalism is the best political system is to prioritize negative liberty, and thereby to abandon strong pluralism of values. Clearly, I cannot delve into this important controversy, as it is not directly connected with the subject matter of this chapter. My aim here was rather to demonstrate that evolutionary theory leads to metaethical realism, which in turn can be gainfully invoked in the argumentation for *ius*-naturalism and against legal positivism.

Epilogue: evil and metaphysics

The main conclusions of this book can be summarized as follows. There are two main reasons why evolutionary theory cannot be used as a basis of construction of a moral system. The first is that evolutionary ethics, that is, ethics expressive of our natural moral propensities, is morally ambivalent – far from being genuine ethics. As I have argued, human beings were endowed by natural selection with moral, neutral and immoral propensities (the first ambivalence of human nature), and the moral propensities (in their basic, that is, evolutionarily shaped form) are themselves ambivalent (the second ambivalence of human nature) – so, for example, human empathy (in its evolutionarily shaped form) is fragile and partial. The second is that evolutionary theory by itself does not provide any guidance for determining whether a given propensity is genuinely moral, ambivalently moral or immoral. The distinction between evolutionary and genuine ethics proved to be useful in two legal-philosophical contexts. It provided a framework for the analysis of progress in law (from the rules corresponding to evolutionary ethics to those corresponding to genuine ethics), and for the construction of an argument for metaethical realism and, indirectly, of an argument for *ius*-naturalism.

The conclusions regarding the nature of evil that are advanced in this book may appear somewhat disappointing. This is partly caused by the profundity of this problem, which probably cannot be fully tackled without going into deeper considerations than evolutionary theory can offer or any scientific theory allows – that is, without going into metaphysical considerations. Let me point out, at the end of this book, two of those deeper, metaphysical aspects of the problem of evil.

First, the ultimate causes of evil behaviour are largely a mystery. It is assumed in this book, contrary to what radical naturalists maintain, that the roots of evil lie in human freedom strongly understood, that is, as freedom of will, being the ability to do (or to have done) otherwise than one really did (which is incompatible with the deterministic picture of the world). But the inquisitive thinker may not be content with stopping here; he may want to ask *why* human beings so often *freely* choose evil. Clearly, a partial answer to this question is provided by those views (for example, the one defended in this book) that point to the propensities of human nature (its *gravity*, to use Weil's wonderfully apt term) that 'push' human beings towards evil. But this answer cannot be interpreted too strongly (deterministically) because it would contradict the assumption of human freedom, which, by definition, enables human beings to overcome their natural limitations. The mystery therefore remains: why, in spite of their knowledge of what is good, do human beings so often freely choose evil? Does freedom of will imply the ability to commit evil acts? These are difficult questions which I cannot deal with here; I shall only limit myself to noting that they receive an illuminating answer from within Christian theology. This answer is that 'it is because of his creaturliness that man is capable of sin' (Pieper 2001: 80). This is a concise summary of Thomas Aquinas' deep analysis of the sources of evil. The analysis in fact has two parts. Its first is the claim that the capability of evildoing is a defect of freedom and, as such, is not part of its essence: 'to sin is a consequence, or even a sign of freedom, but it does not belong to the essence of the free will to be able to decide for evil. The inability to sin should be looked on as the very signature of a higher freedom – possibility for sin is a defect of freedom' (*Summa Theologiae*, 63, 1). The second part (expressed most clearly in Aquinas's treatise *De Veritate*) goes, in Pieper's summary, as follows:

> Not because the will is free but rather because the free will comes from nothing, that is why it is inherent to it not to remain in the good by nature. The freedom may be freedom for the good but not for evil: a free person may be unable to commit evil. A bent toward evil comes to the will not by virtue of its origins from God but because of its origin from nothing ... The creature is dark, insofar as it stems from nothing (i.e. is created). And precisely the fact that descent from nothing is inherent in every creature is the deepest ground for man's capacity for sin, for his *posse peccare*. (Pieper 2001: 81)

Thus, man commits evil because he is free (freedom is, so to say, the *almost*-ultimate cause of evil), but his freedom has the potential for evildoing not because it is freedom but because it is the *defective* freedom of a *created being*, hiding, so to say, nothingness in himself. This answer can, of course, be accepted only by theists; for naturalistically minded thinkers, it will sound extravagant. They may look for the deeper causes of evil (if they find such a search at all necessary) elsewhere; in psychoanalysis, for instance. To give one example of such an answer: Ernst Becker, in his brilliant book *Escape from Evil*, inspired by the thought of the renowned psychoanalyst Otto Rank, asserts that 'man's natural and inevitable urge to deny mortality and achieve a heroic self-image are the root causes of human evil' (Becker 1975: xvii). This hypothesis is, in a way, no less controversial than the theist one. But, in the search for deeper causes of evil, one cannot avoid formulating audacious hypotheses: safe ones illuminate little.

Second, as regards the distinction between evil and goodness, I have basically used three concepts: primary evil (corresponding to our immoral tendencies), secondary evil (generated by our ambivalently moral or neutral tendencies) and goodness (corresponding to actions undertaken in accordance with the rules of genuine ethics). It is clear, however, that in moral evaluation of human actions these distinctions may not prove to be subtle enough and may need to be supplemented by additional considerations. For instance, in Christian moral teaching, two such considerations are taken into account. The first consideration – the relation between the agent's conscience (practical moral judgement) and his actions – enables one to distinguish two levels of evil. One level consists in acting against one's conscience. It is evildoing even if that conscience is in error; as Josef Pieper put it, 'every act of the will is simply and always wrong insofar as it does not agree with reason [i.e., conscience – WZ]' (Pieper 2001: 45). The other level is conscience's being in error. The second consideration is that 'there are two aspects of moral failure: *cupiditas*, which characterizes sin under the viewpoint of turning toward a passing sin, and *superbia*, which characterizes sin under the viewpoint of turning from God' (Pieper 2001: 61–2). The second aspect is more serious: 'the less the concrete deed contains the element of "pride" and the more *cupiditas* it has, the less guiltiness of the action' (Pieper 2001: 62). In the Christian tradition, a sin in which the proportion of *superbia* is so high that it leads to 'turning away' from God is called *peccatum mortale* (mortal sin). But it is also an important element of the Christian theory of *peccatum mortale* that we can never be sure whether a given sinner committed this kind of *peccatum*; what is more, even the sinner himself may not know if he turned away from God (only God knows that). Christianity therefore admits the possibility that no man ever commits *peccatum mortale*. Another interesting point of the Christian theory of *peccatum mortale* is that even the most terrifying deed, for example 'blatantly public violation of lawful order or violation against human dignity' (Pieper 2001: 72), need not be *peccatum mortale*. As noted by Pieper, human beings introduce distinctions between felonies and misdemeanours, serious and trivial offences, but only God knows whether a given human action is a mortal sin. The same evil may be differently evaluated when viewed by men and when viewed by God: 'When looked at from within, the slaying of a human being in the heat of uncontrollable rage might not be a conscious decision against God, while the mere filching of a few cows could very well, under certain conditions, be a decision fraught with eternal consequences' (Pieper 2001: 72). These considerations concerning evil demonstrate that a complete moral evaluation of human actions is extremely difficult, and must take into account such diverse dimensions as the nature of the action itself, its motivation (especially the proportion between *cupiditas* and *superbia*), the action's relation to conscience, and, also, the merit of the agent (that is, the difficulties – for example, one's impulsive personality, which an agent must overcome in order to act morally). My broad distinction between two types of ethics – the evolutionary and the genuine – was focused in the first place on the nature of the action itself and its motivation, and I hope that it shed at least some light on these dimensions. But, needless to say, the distinction could be more nuanced. For instance, in my analysis of genuine ethics I have not considered the possibility that it may consist of various levels of moral perfection. One could argue, for instance, that *highest goodness* transcends what I have called 'genuine ethics', or – more plausibly – constitutes its acme, and thereby an acme of human ethical accomplishment. Illuminating considerations on the issue of highest goodness were proposed by Raimond Gaita, who developed Hannah Arendt's insight that there is 'goodness beyond virtue' and Simone Weil's belief that the highest or purest goodness is not an opposition of evil but is 'above' the opposition of evil and virtue. Gaita (2008: 23, 37) defined 'goodness beyond virtue' as the ability to express 'pure love', to see that each individual is 'unconditionally precious', 'precious beyond reasons, and beyond merit'. I have treated this type of highest goodness as the core part of genuine ethics, though more plausibly it should be viewed as its acme, which, to paraphrase the ending of Spinoza's *Ethics*, is – like all noble things – as difficult to achieve as it is rare.

Bibliography

Aquinas, Thomas, *Summa Theologiae*, www.corpusthomisticum.org.

Arendt, Hannah (1970), *On Violence*, San Diego, New York, London: Harcourt Brace & Company.

Armstrong, Karen (2006), *The Great Transformation: The Beginning of our Religious Traditions*, Toronto: Alfred A. Knopf–Random House.

Axelrod, Robert (1984), *The Evolution of Cooperation*, New York: Basic Books.

Ayala, Francisco (2010), 'What the Biological Sciences Can and Cannot Contribute to Ethics', in: Francisco Ayala and Robert App (eds), *Contemporary Debates in Philosophy of Biology*, Oxford: Wiley-Blackwell, 316–36.

Barberis, Mauro (1998), *L'evoluzione nel diritto*, Torino: g.giappichelli editore.

Baron-Cohen, Simon (2011), *The Science of Evil: On Empathy and the Origins of Cruelty*, New York: Basic Books.

Batson, C. Daniel (1991), *The Altruism Question: Toward a Social-Psychological Answer*, New York: Lawrence Erlbaum Associates.

Becker, Ernst (1975), *Escape from Evil*, New York: The Free Press.

Betzig, Laura L. (2008, 1986), *Despotism and Differential Reproduction: A Darwinian View of History*, New Brunswick and London: Aldine Transaction.

Boehm, Christopher (2001), *Hierarchy in the Forest: The Evolution of Egalitarian Behavior*, Cambridge, MA: Harvard University Press.

Boehm, Christopher (2012), *Moral Origins: The Evolution of Virtue, Altruism, and Shame*, New York: Basic Books.

Broad, Charlie B. (1930), *Five Types of Ethical Theory*, www.ditext.com/broad/ftet/ftet.html.

Buber, Martin (2012), *Je et tu*, transl. G. Bianquis, Paris: Aubier.

Butler, Joseph (2015), *Fifteen Sermons Preached in the Rolls Chapel*, CreateSpace Independent Publishing Platform.

Cameron, Daryl C. and Keith B. Payne (2011), 'Escaping Affect: How Motivated Emotion Regulation Creates Insensitivity to Mass Suffering', *Journal of Personality and Social Psychology*, 100(1), 1–15.

Cartwright, David E. (1988), 'Schopenhauer's Compassion and Nietzsche's Pity', *Schopenhauer Jahrbuch*, 69, 557–67.

de Coulanges, Fustel (1882), *The Ancient City: A Study on the Religion, Laws and Institutions of Greece and Rome*, transl. W. Small, Boston: Lee and Shepard, New York: Charles T. Dillingham.

Daly, Martin and Margo Wilson (1999), *The Truth about Cinderella: A Darwinian View of Parental Love*, New Haven and London: Yale University Press.

D'Arms, John (2008), 'Envy', *The Stanford Encyclopedia of Philosophy*, http://plato.stanford.edu/entries/envy.

Darwin, Charles (1871), *The Descent of Man, and Selection in Relation to Sex*. http://charles-darwin.classic-literature.co.uk/the-descent-of-man.

Dawkins, Richard (1976), *The Selfish Gene*, Oxford: Oxford University Press.

Durkheim, Émile (2011), *O podziale pracy społecznej (De la division du travail social)*, transl. K. Wakar, Warsaw: PWN.

Dziadzio, Andrzej (2008), *Powszechna historia prawa*, Warsaw: PWN.

Dziadzio, Andrzej and Dorota Malec (1997), *Historia prawa. Prawo karne w świetle źródeł*, Krakow: Księgarnia Akademicka.

Eliasz, Katarzyna and Wojciech Załuski (2019), 'Legal Values: Freedom', in: Mortimer Sellers and Stephan Kirste (eds), *Encyclopedia of the Philosophy of Law and Social Philosophy*, Dordrecht: Springer, in press.

Elster, Jon (1999), *Alchemies of the Mind. Rationality and the Emotions*, Cambridge: Cambridge University Press.

Engels, Friedrich (2006, 1884) *L'origine della famiglia, della proprietà private e dello Stato (Der Ursprung der Familie, des Privateigentums und des Staats)*, transl. M. Lentini, Rome: Newton Compton.

Feinberg, Joel (1994), 'Civil Disobedience in the Modern World', in: J. Feinberg, *Freedom and Fulfillment*, Princeton: Princeton University Press, 152–74.

Feinberg, Joel (2002), 'Evil', in: J. Feinberg, *Problems at the Roots of Law: Essays in Legal and Political Theory*, Oxford: Oxford University Press, 125–92.

Finnis, John (1980), *Natural Law and Natural Rights*, Oxford: Oxford University Press.

Freud, Sigmund (1995, 1930), *Kultura jako żródło cierpień (Das Unbehagen in der Kultur)*, transl. J. Prokopiuk, Warsaw: Wydawnictwo KR.

Fuller, Lon L. (1958), 'Positivism and Fidelity to Law: A Reply to Professor Hart', *Harvard Law Review*, 71(4), 630–72.

Gaita, Raimond (2008), *A Common Humanity: Thinking about Love and Truth and Justice*, London and New York: Routledge.

Ghiselin, Michael T. (1974), *The Economy of Nature and the Evolution of Sex*, Berkeley: University of California Press.

Gilligan, James (1997), *Violence: Reflections on a National Epidemic*, New York: Vintage Books.

Gilovich, Thomas, Victoria H. Medvec and Kenneth Savitsky (2000), 'The Spotlight Effect in Social Judgment: An Egocentric Bias in Estimates of the Salience of One's Own Actions and Appearance', *Journal of Personality and Social Psychology*, 78(2), 211–22.

Girard, René (1961), *Mensonge romantique et vérité romanesque*, Paris: Editions Grasset & Fasquelle.

Gizbert-Studnicki, Tomasz (2017), 'Filozofia polityczna a pozytywistyczna teoria prawa', in: A. Bator and P. Kaczmarek (eds), *Przegląd Prawa i Administracji*, Wrocław: Wydawnictwo Uniwersytetu Wrocławskiego, 15–39.

Grabowski, Andrzej (2013), *Juristic Concept of the Validity of Statutory Law. A Critique of Contemprary Legal Nonpositivism*, Berlin, Heidelberg: Springer-Verlag.

Gray, John (2000), *Two Faces of Liberalism*, New York: The New Press.

Green, Leslie (1999), 'Positivism and Conventionalism', *Canadian Journal of Law and Jurisprudence*, 12(1), 35–52.

Hamilton, William D. (1964), 'The Genetical Evolution of Social Behavior, Parts I and II', *Journal of Theoretical Biology*, 7, 1–16, 17–32.

Hart, Herbert L.A. (1958) 'Positivism and the Separation of Law and Morals', *Harvard Law Review*, 71(4), 593–629.

Hart, Herbert L.A. (1994, 1961), *The Concept of Law*, Oxford: Clarendon Press.

Hoftstadter, Richard (1945), *Social Darwinism in American Thought*, Boston: Beacon Press.

Hume, David (1998, 1751), *An Enquiry Concerning the Principles of Morals*, Oxford, New York: Oxford University Press.

Huxley, Thomas (1995, 1894), 'Evolution and Ethics', in: P. Thompson (ed.), *Issues in Evolutionary Ethics*, Albany: State University of New York Press, 111–52.

Jaspers, Karl (2006) *O źródle i celu historii (Vom Ursprung und der Ziel der Geschichte)*, transl. J. Marzęcki, Kęty: Wydawnictwo Marek Derewiecki.

Jedynak, Stanisław (1972), *Etyka Starożytnego Wschodu*, Warsaw: Wiedza Powszechna.

Jenni, Karen and George Loewenstein (1997), 'Explaining the Identifiable Victim Effect', *Journal of Risk and Uncertainty* 14(3), 235–57.

Jones, Owen D. (1997), 'Law and Biology: Toward an Integrated Model of Human Behavior', *Journal of Contemporary Legal Issues*, 8, 167–208.

Jones, Owen D. (2005), 'Evolutionary Psychology and the Law', in: David M. Buss (ed.), *The Handbook of Evolutionary Psychology*, New Jersey: John Wiley & Sons, 953–74.

Jones, Owen D. and Timothy H. Goldsmith (2005), 'Law and Behavioural Biology', *Columbia Law Review*, 105, 405–502.

Joyce, Richard (2000), 'Darwinian Ethics and Error', *Biology and Philosophy* 15, 713–32.

Joyce, Richard (2006), *The Evolution of Morality*, Cambridge, MA: MIT Press.

Kalderon, Mark E. (2005), *Moral Fictionalism*, Oxford: Oxford University Press.

Kant, Immanuel (1986), *Die Religion innerhalb der Grenzen der bloßen Vernunft*, Frankfurt am Main: Suhrkamp Verlag.

Kelsen, Hans (1967), *The Pure Theory of Law*, Berkeley: University of California Press.

Kelsen, Hans (2003, 1953), *Was ist Gerechtigkeit?* Stuttgart: GmbH & Co.

Kelsen, Hans (2017, 1928), *Filozoficzne podstawy nauki prawa natury i pozytywizmu prawnego (Die philosophischen Grundlagen der Naturrechtslehre und des Rechtpositivismus)*, transl. M. Zalewska, Sopot: Arche.

Koestler, Arthur (1975), *The Ghost in the Machine*, London: Picador.

Kuryłowicz, Marek (2006), *Prawa antyczne*, Lublin: Wydawnictwo UMCS.

Levi, Primo (1986), *I Sommersi e I Salvati*, Torino: Einaudi.

Livingstone Smith, David (2007a), *Why We Lie: The Evolutionary Roots of Deception and the Unconscious Mind*, New York: St. Martin's Griffin.

Livingstone Smith, David (2007b), *The Most Dangerous Animal: Human Nature and the Origins of War*, New York: St. Martin's Press.

Lorenz, Konrad (1996, 1983), *Tak zwane zło (Das Sogenannte Böse. Zur Naturgeschichte der Aggression)*, transl. A. D. Tauszyńska, Warsaw: PIW.

Mackie, John L. (1977), *Ethics: Inventing Right and Wrong*, New York: Penguin Books.

Marmor, Andrei (2009), *Social Conventions: From Language to Law*, Princeton: Princeton University Press.

McGraw, Kathleen (1987), 'Guilt Following Transgression: An Attribution of Responsibility Approach', *Journal of Personality Psychology*, 53(2), 247–56.

Mercer, Philip (1972), *Sympathy and Ethics*, Oxford: Oxford University Press.

Midgley, Mary (1997), *Wickedness: A Philosophical Essay*, London and New York: Routledge.

Moore, George. E. (1903), *Principia Ethica*, Cambridge: Cambridge University Press.

Mora, Gonzalo Fernández de la (1987), *Egalitarian Envy. The Political Foundations of Social Justice*, transl. A.T. de Nicolás, New York: Paragon House Publishers.

Nietzsche, Friedrich (1988, 1887), *Zur Genealogie der Moral*, Munich: Deutscher Taschenbuch Verlag de Gruyter.

Old Testament, www.devotions.net/bible.

Petrażycki, Leon (1959), *Teoria prawa i państwa w związku z teorią moralności, Vol. I* , Warsaw: PWN.

Petrażycki, Leon (1960), *Teoria prawa i państwa w związku z teorią moralności, Vol. II*, Warsaw: PWN.

Pieper, Josef (2001, 1977), *The Concept of Sin (Über den Begriff der Sünde)*, transl. E.T. Oakes, South Bend, IN: St. Augustine's Press.

Pietrzykowski, Tomasz (2016), *Ludzkie, niezbyt ludzkie. Esej o podmiotowości prawnej i wyzwaniach XXI wieku*, Katowice: Wydawnictwo Uniwersytetu Śląskiego.

Pinker, Steven (2011), *The Better Angels of our Nature: Why Violence Has Declined*, London: Penguin.

Pizarro, David, Yoel Inbar and Chelsea Helion (2011), 'On Disgust and Moral Judgment', *Emotional Review*, 3(3), 267–8.

Polanowska-Sygulska, Beata (2008), *Pluralizm wartości i jego implikacje w filozofii prawa*, Krakow: Księgarnia Akademicka.

Postema, Gerald (1982), 'Coordination and Convention at the Foundations of Law', *Journal of Legal Studies*, 11, 165.

Raz, Joseph (1979), *The Authority of Law. Essays on Law and Morality*, Oxford: Oxford University Press.

Raz, Joseph (1988), *The Morality of Freedom*, Oxford: Oxford University Press.

Rousseau, Jean-Jacques (1969, 1755), *Discours sur l'origine et les fondements de l'inégalité parmi les hommes*, Paris: Gallimard.

Rozin, Paul. (1999), 'The Process of Moralization', *Psychological Science*, 10(2), 218–21.

Ruse, Michael (1986), *Taking Darwin Seriously: A Naturalistic Approach to Philosophy*, Oxford: Blackwell.

Ruse, Michael (1995), 'Evolutionary Ethics: A Phoenix Arisen', in: Paul Thompson (ed.), *Issues in Evolutionary Ethics*, Albany: State University of New York Press, 225–48.

Ruse, Michael (2006), 'Is Darwinian Metaethics Possible (And If It Is, Is It Well Taken)?', in: Giovanni Boniolo and Gabriele de Anna (eds),

Evolutionary Ethics and Contemporary Biology, Cambridge: Cambridge University Press, 13–26.

Scheler, Max (1980), *Istota i formy sympatii (Wesen und Formen der Sympathie)*, transl. Adam Węgrzecki, Warsaw: PWN.

Scheler, Max (1997), *Resentyment a moralność*, transl. J. Garewicz, Warsaw: Czytelnik.

Schoeck, Helmut (1987, 1969), *Envy. A Theory of Social Behaviour*, Indianapolis: Liberty Press.

Schopenhauer, Arthur (2009), *Die Welt as Wille und Vorstellung*, Vol. I., Köln: Anaconda Verlag GmbH.

Schopenhauer, Arthur (2010), *Die beiden Grundprobleme der Ethik*, Charleston: Nabu Press.

Seneca, *De Ira,* http://www.thelatinlibrary.com/sen/sen.ira1.shtml.

Singer, Peter (1981), *The Expanding Circle: Ethics and Sociobiology*, Oxford: Clarendon Press.

Singer, Peter (1995), *How Are We to Live? Ethics in an Age of Self-Interest*, New York: Prometheus Books.

Slote, Michael (2007), *The Ethics of Care and Empathy*, London and New York: Routledge.

Slovic, Paul (2007), '"If I Look at the Mass I Will Never Act": Psychic Numbing and Genocide', *Judgment and Decision Making*, 2(2), 79–95.

Smith, Adam (2007), *Theory of Moral Sentiments*, New York: Filiquarian Publishing.

Sober, Elliott and David S. Wilson (1998), *Unto Others: The Evolution and Psychology of Unselfish Behavior*, Cambridge, MA: Harvard University Press.

Sójka-Zielińska, Katarzyna (1997), *Historia prawa*, Warsaw: PWN.

Sójka-Zielińska, Katarzyna (2000), *Drogi i bezdroża prawa. Szkice z dziejów kultury prawnej*, Warsaw: Ossolineum.

Spencer, Herbert (1960), *The Man versus the State*, Caldwell, ID: The Caxton Printers.

Strauss, Leo (1965), *Natural Right and History*, Chicago, London: The University of Chicago Press.

Surbey, Michele K. (2004), 'Self-Deception: Helping and Hindering Personal and Public Decision Making', in: Charles Crawford and Catherine Salmon (eds), *Evolutionary Psychology, Public Policy and Personal Decisions*, Mahwah, NJ: Lawrence Erlbaum Associates, 117–44.

Svendsen, Lars (2011), *A Philosophy of Evil*, transl. K.A. Pierce, Champaign, IL and London: Dalkey Archive.

Sykes, Gresham M. and David Matza (1957), 'Techniques of Neutralization: A Theory of Delinquency', *American Sociological Review*, 22(6), 664–70.

Sztompka, Piotr (2007), *Zaufanie. Fundament społeczeństwa*, Krakow: Wydawnictwo Znak.
Tazbir, Janusz (1993), *Okrucieństwo w nowożytnej Europie*, Warsaw: Polska Oficyna Wydawnicza 'BGW'.
Tournier, Paul (1962), *Guilt and Grace: A Psychological Study*, New York: Harper & Row.
Trivers, Robert (1971), 'The Evolution of Reciprocal Altruism', *The Quarterly Review of Biology*, 46(1), 35–57.
Trivers, Robert (2011), *The Folly of Fools: The Logic of Deceit and Self-Deception in Human Life*, New York: Basic Books.
Twain, Mark (2012), *Autobiography of Mark Twain, Vol. I*, Berkeley: University of California Press.
Waal, Frans B.M. de (2006), 'Morally Evolved: Primate Social Instincts, Human Morality, and the Rise and Fall of "Veneer Theory"', in: Stephen Macedo and Josiah Ober (eds), *Primates and Philosophers: How Morality Evolved*, Princeton: Princeton University Press, 1–80.
Weil, Simone (1988, 1947), *La Pesanteur et la Grâce*, Paris: Plon.
Weil, Simone (2017), *La Personne et le Sacré*, Paris: Éditions Payot & Rivages.
Williams, George C. (1966), *Adaptation and Natural Selection: A Critique of Some Current Evolutionary Thought*, Princeton, NJ: Princeton University Press.
Williams, George, C. (1995), 'Huxley's Evolution and Ethics in Sociobiological Perspective', in: P. Thompson (ed.), *Issues in Evolutionary Ethics*, Albany: State University of New York Press, 317–50.
Wilson, Edward O. (1978), *On Human Nature*, Cambridge, MA, London: Harvard University Press.
Wilson, Margo and Martin Daly (1992), 'The Man Who Mistook his Wife for a Chattel', in: J.H. Barkow, L. Cosmides and J. Tooby (eds), *The Adapted Mind: Evolutionary Psychology and the Generation of Culture*, New York: Oxford University Press, 289–322.
Woodruff, Paul (2001), *Reverence: Renewing a Forgotten Virtue*, Oxford: Oxford University Press.
Załuski, Wojciech (2009), *Evolutionary Theory and Legal Philosophy*, Cheltenham, UK: Edward Elgar.
Zdziechowski, Marian (1993), *O okrucieństwie*, Krakow: Znak.

Index